SUCCESS
FROM
SCRATCH

SUCCESS FROM SCRATCH™

MENTAL STRATEGIES FOR SUCCESS IN A SURVIVAL OF THE FITTEST ENVIRONMENT

NICK RUIZ

SOUND WISDOM
P.O. Box 310
Shippensburg, PA 17257-0310

For more information on publishing and distribution rights, call 717-530-2122 or info@soundwisdom.com.,

Quantity Sales. Special discounts are available on quantity purchases by corporations, associations, and others. For details, contact the Sales Department at Sound Wisdom.

While efforts have been made to verify information contained in this publication, neither the author nor the publisher assumes any responsibility for errors, inaccuracies, or omissions.

While this publication is chock-full of useful, practical information, it is not intended to be legal or accounting advice. All readers are advised to seek competent lawyers and accountants to follow laws and regulations that may apply to specific situations.

The reader of this publication assumes responsibility for the use of the information. The author and publisher assume no responsibility or liability whatsoever on the behalf of the reader of this publication.

ISBN 13 TP: 978-1-937879-87-7
ISBN 13 Ebook: 978-1-937879-88-4

For Worldwide Distribution, Printed in the U.S.A.
1 2 3 4 5 6 7 8 / 21 20 19 18 17

Interior design by Terry Clifton
Cover/Jacket designer Eileen Rockwell

CONTENTS

PREFACE

As far back as I can remember, I've loved creating success from nothing—long before I even knew what success was or actually meant. I started my first business when I was in the 4th grade (that I can remember), and I've created dozens of profitable mini businesses ever since. I won't bore you with the details of the first small enterprises, but I *will* share with you the large-scale successes I've created as an adult.

When I look back at all the different business moves I made as a child, the dots fully connect to my business life now. In the moment, I was just a kid doing what I felt compelled to do without much conscious analyzing. It seems I've been a "from scratch" specialist from day one; as an adult, I've created some massive successes. I've also experienced some massive crashes, losing everything. But I'm a thinker and I gain much understanding from every situation. This trait has served me well; and from the wisdom I've gained, I pass it on to you so your quest for success will be smoother than mine was.

CREATING SOMETHING BIG

Right after graduating from high school, I knew I wanted to create something big. I wanted to climb the success ladder as high as I could—I wanted to be financially free. As much as I felt good about all of the mini-successes from scratch I created growing up, it was now time for the serious power moves and paydays.

I enrolled in college because I thought it would lead to a life of success. Halfway into the first semester, I realized it wasn't for me; I wanted to take full control of my journey to success and freedom. Without much thought or hesitation, I dropped out and started working full time. I figured I would work while I built something on the side to gain financial freedom.

One night when I was 19 years old, I watched an infomercial on television about how to buy real estate with no money down. I was young and had no money, and I knew that real estate had made many people very wealthy, so I ordered the program with a credit card. The DVDs and workbooks came in the mail about two weeks later, and I devoured the content. I quickly realized that many of the strategies in the program were pretty farfetched and not very realistic. So, I was discouraged and put it all away for a while.

A few months down the road, I realized how much I needed to get to work on my dreams of building my own empire as an entrepreneur. I had to take action *now*. So I pulled out the real estate materials and grabbed a couple of suggestions that I thought I could execute successfully in my local real estate market—and I took action.

I met with the seller of a home and created a winning deal—he got the price he wanted, and I got the house without any money down. To keep the story short, over the next few years (into my mid-20s), I built a net worth over a million dollars, owned close to 70 buildings, and bought and sold many homes. I had a serious operation going on with lots of people to manage. It happened relatively fast and many lessons were learned—full-blown life lessons, not just business lessons. I was young and had total financial independence and it felt great. I was a millionaire.

There are many lessons-learned events during this time that I could mention, but the ultimate lesson that reshaped my entire world follows.

LOSING EVERYTHING

In 2008, the US experienced the largest market crash since the Great Depression. The mortgage crisis led the way to collapsing the housing market. I had millions in loans that ended up being much higher than the properties were worth—and renters failed to make their monthly payments. There was a perfect storm of many events that eventually collapsed my entire empire. The housing crash eventually forced me into bankruptcy.

I was completely devastated and broke in every sense of the word. I was down to nothing. Mr. Happy Go Lucky was now Mr. Depressed. I wanted to bury myself in a hole and never come out. It is *much* more painful to have money and then lose it all, than to never have had money in the first place. I've been in both scenarios, so I can say that with complete certainty.

I couldn't think straight. My mind was a blur. I had a family to support and questioned the future. I was a man of complete certainty, but after the turn of these events, everything seemed uncertain. I read countless books and programs having to do with personal development and motivation through tough times, but nothing really prepared me for the kind of event I experienced. In fact, I call it a "super experience."

As we age and mature, we get wiser because of our life experiences. Well, when we go through extreme circumstances, it can actually pack decades worth of life experiences and wisdom into a very short period of time. I can say this for sure, now, as I look back, but when I was in the eye of that storm, I didn't see it that way.

Being a successful entrepreneur was intertwined with my identity; because of the bankruptcy, my ego was shattered. What an embarrassment. I was the young, hot shot, successful entrepreneur everyone wanted to learn from— then I was bankrupt. Believe me, my pride could *not* swallow that fact. It was surreal. I didn't want to see anyone; I didn't want to face them and explain. I wanted to protect my identity and the view others had of me. Again, looking back, that should have been the least of my worries; but my immature mindset was in place, and protecting my ego was high on my priority list.

Fortunately, the success psychology was still buried under all that negativity and misery. As my back was against the wall, I dug up the knowledge and drew on my experience and knew that my mind could truly manifest the external world I wanted, even though I was in the midst of total financial, mental, and emotional devastation. I *embraced* the success principles revealed in this book you're holding to reach success at a young age—but after bankruptcy, I *mastered* these proven-successful ideologies and achieved success again and again.

BOUNCE BACK

I bounced back after my bankruptcy in a different way in real estate. I adjusted a few strategies and did things that were much more "economy proof." I won't bore you with all the details of my fast success after bankruptcy, but I will make very clear that my internal world was the foundation of creating it.

In fact, I became so successful so quickly, that I decided to teach people how get into real estate—from scratch. If I could do it from complete knowledge scratch and financial scratch starting in my late teens, and then do it even better right after bankruptcy (with no money and poor credit), I could definitely help a lot of people who were coming from complete scratch.

I wrote a book and titled it *Flip: An Unconventional Guide to Becoming a Real Estate Entrepreneur and Building Your Dream Lifestyle*. I also founded an education company, AlphaHomeFlipping (check out AlphaHomeFlipping.com) that helps people worldwide create wealth and success with real estate. That business also became a wild success. I've sold thousands of books around the world and have sold online courses that have produced many testimonials from everyday people who have had their lives changed from following my principles.

I always knew that real estate entrepreneurship was the best business to start from scratch, but I quickly realized that the online education/information business was a close second. I had an expertise (everyone is an expert at something) and I helped people with that expertise and created a business around that. The beauty of these two specific business models is that you don't need any money or resources to start, you just need to be resourceful and understand the language of success.

I'm not bragging. I just want you to know I can relate to wherever you're coming from. Many "success teachers" have never really been in the financial gutter and so have a relation gap with the people they teach. It's hard to connect with someone who has only been on the upside of things. I've been fully immersed in the "despair" mode. I get you. I get where you're trying to go.

I'm telling you my story because I have a solid track record of creating success from nothing. None of this is fluff and theory that "might work" for you. I've had multiple life-changing scenarios that make me highly qualified to take your hand through this journey through your internal world that will open your eyes to infinite opportunity—infinite opportunity. When your internal world is correct, opportunities will be beating you over the head every day. You want that, right? Of course you do.

Think of this book as a mirror allowing you to view and dissect yourself with perfect precision. You can conduct internal surgery based on what you see in the mirror. Once the surgery is completed, you'll be a custom-built success machine.

SUPPLY AND DEMAND

Let me highlight one more extremely important thing before we start.

I look at every circumstance with a "supply and demand[1] for success" mindset, which allows me to make assessments in a very simplistic way and diagnose and predict scenarios as properly as possible. Nobody has a crystal ball, but this perspective has served me well as an observer.

Fifty to one hundred years ago, ambition was enough to become successful, because almost everyone was trained to be a follower. So back then, an ambitious person could make big things happen with the right actions. Times have changed, though, and many more people want to create their own success to produce the destiny they desire.

You want the edge in this crowded environment, don't you? You want to beat the odds, right? Well, you have to do things differently from today's average motivated and ambitious person if you truly want success.

Before you read further, head over to SuccessFromScratch.net to get the latest updates and bonus content that will put this book on steroids for you. In fact, there is plenty of "success from scratch" content that could not fit into this book, so visit the website as soon as possible.

ENDNOTE

1. Supply and demand is a fundamental concept of economics. "Demand" is how much of a product or service is desired by buyers. "Supply" is how much the market can offer. The relationship between the two is the key to success. More about this topic is found in Chapter 1.

INTRODUCTION

Nowadays, we have no shortage of people teaching others how to be successful. But, more than 90 percent of people who read and take "how to" courses never actually succeed. That's a sad fact. Many people could have the beautiful and successful lives they want, but they are missing key components that actually produce results. At the end of the day, the only thing that matters in your success creation journey, are the results you want.

This book covers creating *real* success from scratch. It doesn't matter if you're at knowledge scratch, financial scratch, or entry-level job scratch level. It doesn't matter if you filed a bankruptcy claim yesterday. In fact, being "at scratch" is perfectly okay because it actually has nothing to do with becoming successful. Where you start from means nothing, as long as you open your mind to the concepts

I share with you that will sculpt the right psychology that produces success and opportunity.

Shaping your external world the way you dream of is 100 percent doable. I'm fully certain of that. I'm personal proof, along with many other people in the world who have achieved their success goals. The issue is that most people have an *internal* world and perception that prevents them from experiencing success. They point to all that's wrong with the *external* world around them—the circumstances they were born into, lack of education, where they live, etc.,—and use those things as excuses to explain why they aren't where they want to be in life. They are always running into brick walls and dead ends.

Success opportunities may be presented to you every day, but each one may be in a language you don't understand. The principles in this book teach you how to become fluent in the language of success and opportunity, so you can step into the world and receive with full clarity and understanding.

Throughout this book, you are introduced to a higher level of thinking and perception that transcends the traditional "hustle, hustle" and "work 24 hours a day till you succeed" kind of thinking. You may have heard how you have to outwork your competitors and sleep three hours per night to succeed. I'm not discounting the fact that you must make sacrifices to create success, but recalibrating your internal world to match the external world you want to create is very important.

THE LANGUAGE OF SUCCESS AND OPPORTUNITY

Do you know people who are "lucky" and things always seem to go their way? Actually, they aren't lucky—they are fluent in the language of success and opportunity. They have developed a very sharp lens through which they see the world, and they notice opportunities that most people look right past.

Many gurus say to take massive action to create massive results. I'll be the first to tell you that taking lots of action is necessary, but there are plenty of people taking insane amounts of action and getting little to no results. Again, success is not just taking action, it is having the right mindset and following a few important principles.

This book isn't a step by step, do this and do that manual. For example, everyone knows exactly the steps to becoming physically fit—1) eat less and healthier foods and 2) exercise regularly. Those are only *two* steps, and most people are still unsuccessful at losing weight.

The principles in this book will reshape your thinking process that, most likely, has been shaped by default as the result of experiences, external circumstances, and people around you. It's time for you to consciously take control of your mental processes and perceptions. My goal is for you to walk away from reading this book with a reshaped internal world and perception of the world that will inevitably produce the successful external circumstances and events you want to achieve.

GOOD NEWS

The good news: First, *your mind and your whole world is one big ball of moldable clay.* It doesn't matter where you are currently or where you came from. Success isn't partial to any specific race, gender, age, nationality, family history, etc. There is no debating that fact, especially considering how many worldwide, unique rags-to-riches success stories there are. "Rags" motivate.

I've been at scratch multiple times, and hindsight is 20/20. I can look back at my successes and my downfall with complete clarity from an objective point of view. You don't need decades to fulfill your dreams. You need the principles I share with you; you may have never been conscious of the fact that you aren't embracing these principles and perceptions. After you read the last page of this book, you'll be fully conscious of the areas you need to work on, and the power to succeed will be in the palm of your hands. You can sculpt your internal world so the external world becomes one big opportunity. That's pretty exciting!

You can embrace being at scratch because it gives you a built-in shortcut to reshaping your internal world and perceptions, almost out of necessity. You don't have time to go through the motions, overthink things, and paralyze yourself with "what if" type of thoughts. You become resourceful, and your instincts for success take over.

In fact, that's my second bit of good news: *success is already hardwired in you.* It's part of your nervous system. Think about toddlers. They continually stand up and try to walk. Even though they fall, they naturally continue to get up and try to walk. They don't need their parents to convince them to do it or push them, they automatically try and try again. After the 100th try when they still fall, their parents don't say, "Oh well, I guess little Jimmy isn't going to be a walker." No! Walking *will* happen. It's a certainty.

The beauty is that we already have inside of us what it truly takes to create success. The unfortunate reality is that as we mature from early childhood, the external world shapes our minds, brains, and nervous systems to where we are completely "taught out" of success. It's a shame, but it's part of this world we live in.

I would venture to say that none of the principles provided in this book are taught in schools; that's why only a small percentage of the total population actually succeed to the level they desire. The structure the world operates within is built to produce followers. As we mature, it's our responsibility to consciously reshape our minds and perceptions to those that make success natural and almost automatic. It isn't always easy—especially if you're in a bad environment that doesn't nurture your progress—but it is entirely possible.

SELF-AWARENESS AND SELF-RELIANCE

One of the most crucial traits of successful people (whether they know it consciously or not) is the fact that they are *self-aware* and constantly adapting and recalibrating their internal world to the continuing success they are creating for themselves. On top of that trait, another key trait is that of *self-reliance*. They don't think about all of the resources they *don't* have—they become resourceful with what they *do* have.

My obsession has always been to deconstruct and dissect situations, opportunities, conversations, relationships, etc. to find the deepest possible understanding. It's best to ask yourself: *Why do birds (people) of a feather (mindset) flock together? What are the psychological benefits and repercussions of being around people like me? What if I'm the wrong kind of person and being around others like me only makes my life go farther in the wrong direction, and I'm not even aware? What if the people around me are validating my mediocre behaviors that are not working in my best interest?*

When you have a broader perception and deeper understanding of the language of success and opportunity, you'll be at a place where you can actually create the success you want. You would *survive* in a foreign country without knowing a word of the language. But if you become fluent in that language before you arrive, you will successfully *thrive*.

As much as you think your success depends on what you do and say, the people you meet, and books you read, I'm here to tell you that *recalibrating your mind and perception is the foundation of the success sequence.* If you understand this and implement what you are about to read, then the things you need to do and say to create success will feel almost effortless.

Let's continue...

1

THE NEW HERD

In my opinion, today's society is much more attuned to critical thinking and questioning than in years past. No doubt we can name Albert Einstein and other great thinkers, but today we can name many more—because of the inventions and the groundwork of previous successes.

Nowadays, the supply and *demand* for success has shifted, and more and more people are raising their hands saying, "Hey, I want success too, what do I have to do?" One thing I've learned over my lifetime of creating success from scratch, building businesses, etc., is that supply and demand spills over into all parts of society. I try to have a "zoomed-out approach" that allows me to objectively look with a "supply and demand" mentality of current and future events. As stated previously, I don't have a crystal ball, but I can understand shifts in society, culture, people, and business and can anticipate and stay ahead of the masses.

The *supply* of opportunities for success is high. There also is a high demand and only a small window to get the supplied success that's available. The same general principles to gain success are being used by the masses, which means there has to be an evolutionary shift. That's why this book reveals the wisdom of sculpting your internal world into a way that you can access the supplied success.

The supply of people who want success is higher than ever because of the Internet and new and different platforms that allow people to gain access to information. Information is the most valuable commodity in the world. There's nothing more valuable than information; and because of the ease of accessing information, more people are realizing, "Hey, if I critically think about things and change this and that, I can be one of the successful few instead of a member of the herd."

Fifty to one hundred years ago, the only information people had was what was told to them by their parents, teachers, bosses, and other authority figures, which never led them to question:

"How can I meet that need?"

"Can I have more?"

"What can I do to have more?"

"How can I help others in a significant way?"

"Can this be done differently?"

"Is this all there is?"

For many people back then, it was ingrained from the beginning that they should accept things as they are and there is no sense in questioning, because nothing was going to change. Today, the masses want success and are becoming the "New Herd." Consequently, you have to be over and above the common stream of thought and have a higher level of thinking.

The continual supply of information to create success is becoming part of the mass's mentality. But a lot of it is recycled and general knowledge. It's the same basic "work harder than everyone else" mindset. To rise above the crowds, you must re-sculpt your internal world in a unique way and revisit the perceptions you have. The psychologies that have been literally ingrained into your hardwiring since you've been born need to be questioned. You need to create your inner world and perceptions in a conscious way.

ABOVE THE FRAY

Because of unprecedented technology advancements and social media, average people can see firsthand how successful people live and the successes they create. Since everything is so much more visible and "in your face" these days, more and more people are saying, "Hey, I want that life!" That's okay, but this phenomenon is developing a herd within itself, so we need to stay ahead and above the fray by adjusting our thinking and actions.

In the following chapters, you will learn how to reach the higher mind and perceptions level that gains success. The key is to clearly recognize and understand this new herd, and operate at a level above. I can't stress enough that the amount of people racing into the world of wanting and demanding success is so high that we have to shift our actions and mentalities to separate ourselves to create success.

Separating yourself from the masses is clear and simple. I didn't say *easy,* though. It will take time, effort, and energy on your part; but after you understand what it takes to have a higher mind, a different perception, and an opportunistic viewpoint, you'll be in a much better place and move in a different direction from the masses.

Each of the following individual principles and ideologies presented separates and elevates you to a "three dimensional" approach to success. We will also deeply dive into self-reflection and understanding of what's preventing you from achieving success or how you achieved your current success and how to keep it.

The new herd is here, so be ready, be prepared, and engage in the ideas moving forward in this book. Because I know you want to stand out and really understand success at the highest level, there are free resources for you at SuccessFromScratch.net.

2

SUCCESS IS "TAUGHT OUT" OF US

Humans, along with many other species, naturally know how to succeed from birth. It's an instinct. We don't stop until we get what we set out to get. This urge comes from survival instincts embedded deeply within us. Remember the toddler example. In fact, children are trial-and-error masters. They understand trying, changing, and evolving strategies better than any adult because they haven't been "taught out" of it yet. We don't stop exploring new things until we are told of danger. We are told not to do things for one reason or another. Many of the reasons can be good, but there are a *lot* that don't actually serve us well as we mature.

Thankfully, our brains can be rewired, which is a total blessing because we can consciously recreate the way our brain works to achieve anything we want. We can create any kind of traits we desire. Seriously. If you don't like things about yourself, habits you have, or how you behave, you can hack into your nervous system and makes changes.

The downside to your brain being able to be rewired is that our brains can be shaped in the negative direction by external stimuli over which we have no control. We turn out the way we turn out because external events, people, and circumstances have shaped us in ways in which we don't even have a conscious realization. We start out as children who have infinite imaginations ready to explore and engage in constant curiosity. Everything around is full of wonder and we are constantly trying to explore with as many senses as possible.

Then, as we mature, we realize there is danger in the world and the adults around us try to protect us, as they should. There is a line that needs to be drawn, though, for our protection. Obviously we want to be safe from extreme situations that can lead to death or devastating outcomes, but it's okay to get scraped knees. In fact, when my daughters come to me with minor scratches from playing outside, I remind them that it means they were having a lot of fun. This simple principle should extend into our adulthood, but it doesn't.

When we become too protected and are told to stop being curious and touching things, we start to develop a new set of hardwired behaviors. In fact, enough repetition of anything results in new, automatic behaviors. This happens on a physiological level. New pathways in the brain develop; and the more the behavior is repeated, the more it gets cemented into an automatic action. This is the basis of any type of habit creation. I believe that we were born to succeed at whatever internal interest was embedded in us—and the world around us slowly teaches us out of it because it doesn't seem safe or realistic.

Our parents, siblings, cousins, aunts, uncles, friends, teachers, etc. have slowly shaped our behaviors and habits so that we stay safe and conform with the common objective of long-term security. This agenda includes earning good grades; going to college to get a degree in a field with good-paying, secure jobs; work your way up; and retire with a pension. I'm not knocking getting a job. What I'm knocking is doing something you hate just for a Friday paycheck. I look at it as trading your everyday happiness for a weekly paycheck. That's not a good exchange if you ask me.

The *correct* exchange I want for you is to achieve success to the point where you can use money to buy time and freedom. That's the exchange that most people look at and wonder how the "lucky few" were able to achieve it. This book is all about teaching you how to be part of that few.

REBOOT AND REINSTALL

We are products of our consistent environment, and also our childhood and past. Whatever you do, don't just think, "I was a kid, and now I'm grown up and much wiser." No! There are embedded patterns deeply engrained into your nervous system from your *very* early ages. Don't believe me? There are millions of adults in their 30s, 40s, 50s, 60s, and beyond who go through intense therapy to unravel events from their childhood. Some have experienced catastrophic life events that they haven't overcome and have been living in fear and in an anxiety-ridden, paralyzed state for decades. This is proof that your early years matter a lot.

I want to focus on the less traumatic early-life conditioning, on the events, circumstances, and people that look like no big deal, but really are the building blocks and part of operating system that influence most people's daily activities and behaviors.

Your nervous system is your operating system, and your behaviors are the outputs. Your internal operating system may need to be slightly defragmented—clean up or clean out unwanted and unnecessary data. Or, you may need a total reboot and reinstall. The point is, no matter where you are, it's okay because I will show you how to consciously understand where you are and where you come from so you know how to proceed in the direction you want, instead of the direction you're headed toward by default.

Your brain (the headquarters of your nervous system) looks out for painful events and creates a connection afterward to make sure you don't go down that route again for your protection. It also releases reward hormones when you do something that it likes. The simplest, classic example is being burned. When a child touches a hot stovetop and gets burned, the brain makes a connection that stovetops equal pain. It may take a few more painful lessons to really get embedded, but then it's a permanent pathway in the brain. Children will automatically avoid stovetops, candle flames, hot irons, etc. moving forward because they know pain is the result of touching it.

Another example, a 6-year-old who likes to dig for worms and play in the mud. Time and time again his parents yell at him to stop getting dirty and stop playing with slimy, filthy worms. After days and weeks of going out and doing what he's naturally drawn to do, his desire starts to fade because of the reprimands. His brain automatically starts to measure the worth of all the yelling and punishments that come after he goes outside to do what he loves. His parents think they are looking out for him by keeping him clean. They think they are teaching him a life lesson of being clean and staying safely away from dirt, mud, and slimy creatures.

Now, if the child has a very strong interest in worms, it may take longer to condition him to stay away from the mud. It may take months of his parents yelling at him before he really starts to change his behavior. The point: his behavior toward his natural interest *will* be changed because of the negativity associated with it, created by an outside force (his parents). His brain will tell him, "It's not worth being yelled at and punished. Maybe I'm better off staying away from that stuff." This is reinforced even further because kids have a natural tendency to trust what adults say is best for them. They think, "If my mom (dad, aunt, uncle, etc.) says it's not good, then it probably isn't."

Now in this very simple illustration, I'm not saying that his parents had any ill intent whatsoever. I'm simply saying that this is one very small and easy illustration that shows us how our behavior starts to shape as we get older. Who knows, maybe if the parents nurtured and recognized this child's natural gravitation toward worms and fully embraced it, he could've been one of the world's top worm experts. The thing that people are truly born to be might never see the light of day because of external forces with good intentions.

When you have a conscious awareness of things discussed here, a whole new world awaits your arrival. And you will be like a kid in a candy store for the rest of your life. In fact, what is "a kid in a candy store"? He or she is someone who looks around and sees nothing but opportunities to be happy. You will be someone who can look in any direction and perceive and achieve pleasurable experiences.

When you realize that your actions up to this point have been created by everyone and everything else but you, you can finally approach the world in a way that allows you to be a kid in a candy store. The only thing stopping you from the success you desire is the mindset that you've developed from years of conditioning.

REFLECTING ON YOUR PAST, CREATING YOUR FUTURE

Now, think about your past and what you've been told by people around you (even people very close to you). Think about what your parents have taught you about success. Maybe your parents think, or thought, there's only a lucky few who get to be successful, and everyone else has to accept being average. Most people have a "This is as good as it gets" mentality. They believe that life has limits and where you are now is probably where you were meant to be, and no more.

I couldn't have a fiercer opposition to this thinking. But I also understand why they have those beliefs. They are derived from their own past conditioning. That's why poverty is usually generational. It takes someone to raise a hand and realize that what was before is not a pre-written story that has to be played out. Once you wake up to the fact that necessary behavioral changes can be made, you have a blank script in front of you—and you're the writer. The only limit is your imagination.

I'm not saying that breaking these kinds of generational patterns is easy, but you do have the most powerful machine in the universe sitting right behind your eyes that are reading these words, waiting for you to take control. Just because your brain has unfathomable power doesn't mean it's automatically going to go in the positive direction with that power. It's up to you to continually guide it. Yes, *continually*. The success journey never ends. It's an infinite climb that should bring satisfaction through all of its stages.

The reality is that you are going against physiological realities. There are real pathways in the brain that have been developed over time and can actually be measured and seen on a brain scan. These are not just "mind things" that you need to get over. You can actually change the structure of certain parts of your brain.

Now, it's time to create a custom environment around you with the right people and events that cater to and complement your desired, successful state of mind. You may need to make adjustments in your current stage of relationships—you want to surround yourself with a circle of people who bring you to success. You want people with the success psychology through and through. You want people who are always smiling and optimistic. You want people who don't start most of your conversations with some type of complaint.

The new people you start surrounding yourself with will change your way of thinking. They are changing your viewpoint and the way you perceive external stimuli. When you look at what's happening, you will see unique opportunities that you've never seen before. You will start to mirror the expectations and standards that these people have for themselves. You don't want to feel pain, so you will make sure you're fitting in by taking the types of actions they take.

Remember, the beginning will be tough, but you are creating real pathways in your brain that will become developed over time until the positive mindset and actions happen almost unconsciously. You won't even have to think about doing the things that you once thought were so foreign. After time, the positive mindset, the successful actions, and the opportunistic viewpoint will be part of who you are.

When you have created this new environment around you, new events will start to happen. More opportunities will come your way. Somehow, there will be much less for you to complain about. More like-minded people will start to cross paths with you. Remember, I told you that the people, events, and circumstances to this date have been what has given you your perception and viewpoint on what's acceptable. So now, new events will occur.

You'll be promoted at your job because the boss sees an optimistic, action-taking powerhouse who is making all the right moves. All your relationships will improve and become more stimulating and fun. Your new business ideas will take off because of all of the new opportunities you see that you used to be blind to. This turns into an exponentially positive cycle of events that shape and cement your new mindset even more. Do you see the importance of crafting your own environment?

The whole point of this chapter is for you to open your eyes and look back and really understand where your viewpoints and habits come from. We are born with a general brain architecture that has some built-in settings, but much of what we are today has been developed over time. We have to realize this or we are dead in the water when it comes to creating success.

Next you will see how to sculpt your inner success factory; but until you realize that most of your ways are based on how you've been guided by the influential people in your life, you won't be able to properly engage in your necessary redevelopment.

Now, on to the next principle...

3

Your Success Is a Unique, Evolutionary Process

Each person has a unique set of DNA. Each person has a unique set of experiences, along with external events and people and things to which they've been exposed. That combination is, literally, one in infinity, because there is only one set of that exact combination that ever has and that ever will be in all of existence.

It is vitally important to look internally to see your strengths and recognize your weaknesses. When you are self-aware, you will slowly experience your own unique evolutionary process to create success that can and will look completely different from everyone else's process.

I caution you not to try to step-by-step duplicate some-one else's success journey. I'm a fan of picking bits and pieces from other people's journeys to use for our benefit for shortcuts. But trying to copy someone exactly will hin-der your unique proposition to the world—which is *you*. The only way to truly succeed in a fulfilled way is to under-stand yourself, what you're good at, what you're not good at, understand the marketplace, and understand the industry in which you're trying to succeed. Then just be you and pur-sue success on your terms that coincide with your being.

In the early days of my entrepreneurial career, I recol-lect multiple times when I saw people on seats of success and thought, *I want to be like that. I want that. I want my success to look like that.* But what that mindset and intensity actually did was force me into *their* process and *their* jour-ney, which took away from my unique abilities. Many of my unique abilities may have been put on the back burner without me even knowing because I was so immersed in duplicating someone's success path and success journey.

There is a distinct difference between modeling and completely duplicating and emulating someone's suc-cess journey. Nowadays, one touch of a computer or smart phone screen and we can see people's successes and pictures of their nice houses and cars. So much information is acces-sible today. A lot of people say, "That's what I want! I need to find out exactly, step by step, what they did to get there. Did they raise money and start a tech company? Well, that's what I want to do." Guess what? Raising money and build-ing a tech company may oppose your unique greatness and unique skill sets, causing you to unnecessarily waste time.

Yes, you'll learn from that mistake, but I want to help you shorten that learning curve.

STRENGTHS AND WEAKNESSES

What you do to gain success has to coincide with who you are and what your strengths and weaknesses are. I know my weaknesses. I don't try to develop those into strengths because there isn't enough time in the world for me to do that. I focus where I'm strong. Yes, I model and emulate successful people and pull out strategies that they've used, but I work on building businesses that coincide with Nick and who I am as a person, and what I'm best at. I build a team around my weaknesses.

Everyone's strengths and weaknesses are a little different, so how could we possibly think about duplicating the path of someone who created some type of success when they have their own strengths and weaknesses. Every path of success is uniquely different, and it evolves organically in your own way based on your DNA and your life experiences.

Once you gain the internal awareness of your strengths and weaknesses and start to develop your own evolution of your path to success, it's important to go places where your agenda and your strengths are nurtured. You don't want to hear people say, "Oh, well you have to do it this way. You're weak here; you better become strong because you're going to need that if you want to become successful." You don't need to be strong across the board. Stay far away from negative people. You need to go where you're nurtured, like evolution in nature. You want to be with people who confirm what you're doing, confirm your strengths, confirm the evolution that's coming about in you—it will exponentially grow your path to success.

Right now you're on the first step of the staircase. You know what it looks like. It's exciting to think about what the twentieth step on the top will look like. But you're not in the state of consciousness yet that can understand what the twentieth stair looks like. But if you open your mind to allow your unique self to constantly evolve, chances are you will be totally thrilled with how your life will turn out.

Being extremely open-minded allows for a much healthier evolutionary path on your journey to success. So many people want to plot out their entire path all the way to the mansions and Lamborghinis, and every step it's going to take to get there. I very much oppose this kind of psychology and recommend that you go against it. It creates tunnel vision, which hinders great opportunities, events, exposures, and meeting people you don't even know exist yet. It's okay to have big goals. I understand that. But to plot out the entire journey is a disservice because there is so much out there that your present state of mind doesn't know about or even understand. Evolutionary growth produces that understanding one step at a time. You have to be open-minded in order to let your journey flow organically.

If you want to hear some in-depth talks that go really raw and deep into this evolutionary process, visit Success-FromScratch.net to get into some really interesting content.

4

WHAT LENSES ARE YOU WEARING?

Whether you're running into brick walls regularly or you're running into opportunities regularly, or any situation in between, it all has to do with what lenses you're wearing, what your perception is, how you see the world. How you see the world has been shaped by your past experiences. A lot of events in your life that are completely neutral end up being viewed as positive or negative, based on the lenses you're wearing.

Do you view the world through opportunistic or pessimistic lenses? The world is going to fulfill how you see it. That's how it works.

Your surrounding environment will consistently give you more of what your perception produces. If you're constantly viewing things in a negative way and looking at everything that's wrong, then that's what you will regularly experience. Your negative world will remain a constant and fulfill itself automatically every single day. That's a mentally dangerous place to be and it all can stem from the perceptions you've developed over the past years of your life. Consciously choosing the lens you look out of is the only way to ensure good things cross your path consistently.

To highlight this a little more, I like to use an analogy about the lens comedians use. Comedians have the ability to see "funny" in places that the average person doesn't. They can see a dozen funny things just while getting their groceries. Their comedic lens allows them to see what others would never see. They've shaped their eyes to see funny things in neutral situations.

Once you understand that simple analogy, you'll easily be able to see how the opportunistic lens and the pessimistic lens work the same way. If you've developed over time (whether consciously or unconsciously) the pessimistic lens, you're going to see nothing but brick walls, unlucky "situations," and bad things. You'll feel like nothing goes your way.

On the flipside, if you've developed the opportunistic lens, you see nothing but upside. Even when things are negative, you see an upside. You see that there are opportunities under your nose everywhere you turn because of your viewpoint and perception. The key: most situations and events in life are neutral; the lens you see them through makes all the difference in whether your personal reality is positive or negative.

I've always had more of an opportunistic lens. A lot of that was questioned and really challenged when I went through my hard times financially. I remember asking myself questions that I never thought I would ask. Temporarily, I had a pessimistic point of view and asked myself, *Was that my shot and it didn't work out? Was this the one shot I had at succeeding and now it's back to a regular, schmucky old life?*

As successful, optimistic, and opportunistic as I was, those thoughts definitely were in my mind. When going through a devastating financial or personal scenario, negativity can spiral quickly. Negativity can compound harder and faster than positivity. I think that's how we are wired as humans—downfalls and negativities happen faster and harder than upsides. Upsides, most of the time, take more work. Reflecting on my most devastating scenario, I wouldn't say I developed a pessimistic lens, but I would say that my optimistic lens was drastically challenged. I remember thinking, *Oh my gosh, everywhere I turn this bad thing is happening or that trouble is happening. What's next?!* Thankfully it didn't last long because of the psychology I had developed, which allowed me to quickly bounce back.

A major key to understand is that the lens most people have has been developed over a long period of time, whether a comedian, an opportunistic person, or a pessimistic person. Make no mistake about it, some environments are more favorable than others to our success in whatever we're trying to achieve. It's critical to be aware of why and how you see life.

Changing your lens is not easy when you've been conditioned a certain way for such a long time. Step one to getting the right viewpoint and perception is to be aware of your lens. Most people coast through life for months, years, decades, or their whole lives, without realizing that the majority of what appears negative is because that's how they view the world. At this stage in your journey, I want to shake you so you wake up and say, "Hey, maybe I am where I am in life because of how I see everything and *not* because of my past or current environment or circumstances."

WHERE ARE YOU?

To make any change, you must understand where you currently are. You can't change what you don't know currently exists. You can't get sober until you understand and admit that you're an addict, otherwise you don't even know the need to become sober. The change can come after that with the right strategies and processes.

There are certain events in our lives that allow us to recognize how we've been seeing things. It's a matter of reflecting on what's happened in your past life and your current life and how you react to certain scenarios. Upon reflection, you will most likely see a pattern that perhaps you were not aware of. Becoming conscious and aware is step one to all success.

Successful people are open-minded. You have to have an open mind, or at least open enough to admit your shortcomings, admit where you stand, and even talk to other people about how you see things. Maybe family and friends have noticed your pessimistic or negative mindset, but were afraid to tell you because they didn't want to hurt your feelings.

A positive approach and exercise to approach people who love and care about you the most is to ask them outright, "Do you see me as a pessimistic person, an opportunistic person, or a positive-lensed person? How do you think I see the world?" Hopefully, they will give you honest and straight answers; but if you're closed-minded, you will be defensive and reject what you don't want to hear.

Becoming successful involves an element of maturity to where you are open to the right types of criticisms that allow you to see yourself. Because you're immersed in yourself, inside your own head and body 24/7/365, you don't have an objective point of view that outsiders have. It's like when you hear your voice from a recording. It sounds different to you because you're hearing it from outside yourself. That's how your mental world works as well. You might think, *This is the way life is. I'm not pessimistic. I'm not looking through the wrong lens. This is just the star I was born under and the events that were laid out for me from a prewritten script.*

Your whole life can be drastically altered in a positive way, but if you're not conscious of it, it'll never change, and it will always look like doom and gloom because you've never questioned your own perceptions.

Many people have a tough time handling criticism and outside observations of themselves. I can't stress enough that stubbornness and closed-mindedness will kill your chances for success faster than you can imagine. I've been stubborn in many life scenarios, and looking back I wish I was more open-minded. As I've matured and developed over the years as a person and as an entrepreneur, I'm now usually open-minded enough to hear anything, and then I can decide if it's accurate or if it's something that could help me or hurt me.

SUPPORT OR SABOTAGE

Unfortunately, there are people who would love to either support or sabotage your success, so you have to be able to decipher one from the other. If you tell me you can fly to the moon and back on a bicycle, let's have lunch. I'll hear about it. I might not believe it or accept it, but I'm open-minded enough to hear it and maybe pull 1 percent out of it that I've never heard before and it could be a seed that takes off in its own direction once it's planted in my brain. I think that's what allows greatness and success to be achieved—nothing is off limits. Talk to me. I'll hear you.

The "macro lenses" of success are opportunistic and optimistic lenses on one side, and pessimistic and fearful lenses on the other side. Those are the four basic denominators, then there are various "micro lenses" within those four basic macro lenses. If your lenses are on the negative side, the world will not appear very welcoming. You will see everyone else succeeding and enjoying life. To have good things happen to you, you *must* view the world through the correct lenses—opportunistic and optimistic.

The movie *Life Is Beautiful* is a perfect example of seeing the world through an optimistic lens. The story centers on a Jewish father and son who were rounded up with others and put in a train that took them to a concentration camp. This period in Europe was one of the most devastating times in human history. Hitler wanted to exterminate the Jews—and the people in the camp knew they would eventually be killed. The father held on to hope and chose to make the environment for his son one of positivity and happiness. Each day he would create imaginative stories and create a positive lens for the young boy to look through. In the depths and darkness of what happens in concentration camps, this child saw life only through the lens that his father held before him—one of adventure, possibility, opportunity, and happiness. Even though the situation was tortuous, bleak, and deadly, the young boy could smile because his father gifted him with an optimistic lens through which to see life.

Unlike the tragic circumstances of a concentration camp, most of us today deal with trivial, inconsequential neutral situations that we cry and complain about. We look at them as devastating and negative and unlucky, but most of them are just neutral problems that look larger than they are because we're looking at them from the wrong vantage point.

IMAGINATION AND OPTIMISM

Let's look at two facts. First: Our imaginations are infinite. What we can create in our minds is not even fathomable. We have no idea the capabilities of our own minds, even as technologically and medically advanced as we are. The world we can create inside of us can trump anything that's happening externally. Second: Choosing to be around positive, opportunistic, and optimistic people on a regular basis will eventually change the lens you look through. If you are already looking through the correct lens, your outlook will be strengthened.

But if you're on the other side of the spectrum and feel like you're running into brick walls every day, thinking life isn't fair and you're getting treated unfairly (which may absolutely be true), you are going to have a whole different experience of opportunity in life. If you associate with positive-thinking people, you'll start to feel like you are in control, and opportunity will be everywhere. There will be opportunity for happiness, opportunity for success, opportunity for career advancement, etc. when you're around people who see their worlds that way.

One of the best success strategies in the world—choose to be around positive people.

If you don't like to reach out to others but you want to reach success, you have to go outside your comfort zone to change your lens. If you're not used to this type of interaction, it is going to be uncomfortable for you at first. You may have to make a scary phone call or write an email that makes you vulnerable or causes possible rejection. But listen—that one small move can open doors and plant seeds that are beyond anything you can even imagine.

I'm all about one small move getting one small result and then exponentially expanding from there. I'm all about the acorn producing a forest, and it can happen quickly. You don't need a lifetime, decades, or even one decade for something significant to happen. After one positive result, have your brain reward you. After earning more positive results, your brain will reward you further, until from head to toe you have restructured your entire existence piece by piece.

It doesn't have to be a lifelong journey to change your perceptions and lenses. You may have the right lens already and are looking to grow more. Or, you may have a completely wrong lens that has been developed over the years of your life. Your environment trumps all. If you're around people who are wearing the correct lenses, osmosis happens very quickly.

Also, open-mindedness drastically enhances and shortens your personal growth curve in this area. Remember the importance of hearing everyone out. You never know what kind of gold can be mined from the most unusual and unexpected places. It's human nature to reject what we don't know or what we don't understand. But the simple reality is that everything you want is in territory you haven't been in yet, so of course it's foreign. But if *you* are open, the floodgates open.

5

CARROT AND STICK

I don't think humans have changed much since the beginning of time. Our lives center on incentives and repercussions. We do things because rewards are attached, and then we don't like the consequences for things we do wrong, or things we neglect to do. It's in our primitive nature and hardwired into us. We must understand that the carrot (reward) and the stick (punishment) are the two main aspects of life that shape our behavior and how we operate.

If your incentives aren't big enough and visible enough to you, you won't take the necessary actions to reach your goal. Also, if the pain and repercussions aren't real enough to prevent you from doing wrong things or neglecting to do the right things, then you won't eliminate those actions in your life.

We've been shaped over the years on the principle of the carrot and stick. You need to understand this so you can consciously start shaping your actions. Otherwise, again, default will take over and the external world will shape your behaviors. Success involves creating your own conscious behavior, as opposed to the environment creating your behaviors for you.

NEW INCENTIVES

How do we establish new incentives? Incentives are established by understanding, seeing, and being exposed to things that you want. Many people are immersed in environments that are not beneficial for our success because they don't expose us to what we could have or what we could be. Again, that goes back to the default shaping that happens unconsciously, and that's why it's so poisonous to be immersed in the wrong environment. Usually we aren't consciously aware that we are in the wrong environment, which can be very scary.

For example, a fish doesn't know it's in a sea of water. Humans don't consciously think that we're in a sea of oxygen simply because we can't see it. Our eyes don't allow us to see the oxygen, but it's there. This is a simple analogy showing that we could be immersed in a sea of negativity and failure-producing environments without knowing it.

Establishing new incentives involves creating a new environment, including people, events, and circumstances in your life. Once you establish a new surrounding of people, the events in your life will change. When the events in your life change, you'll react differently based on the people you're around. When you react differently, the entire surrounding circumstances of your life will change. Then you will experience an uphill and upward spiral that will continue and grow exponentially.

We don't have the right incentives in front of us because we are not consciously aware of what we want. That's the beginning step. First establish what you want, and then create mini goals and incentives along with macro goals and incentives for the long term.

For the most part, humans do only what they have to do. Obviously, there are exceptions to that rule and those are the people who are most successful. For example, when you're working out and bench pressing by yourself, when you get to the number you decided on, you stop. But if a trainer tells you to do three more reps over the number, you're going to do them because of a simple environmental change like a trainer. The beauty of those three extra reps is that most success and change happens in those last three reps that take extra effort, not the first twenty that felt comfortable.

My point? Success and magic happens with extra effort. Because most people's environments are incorrect and we do only what we have to do, based on our human nature, we seldom experience the true growth and success we want.

EXTRA EFFORT

If you are in despair and in pain and desperation, down to zero or broke or depressed, embrace your current situation. I can say that with clarity because I've been there, and looking back, with hindsight being 20/20, it works and it's something you must do. When you're in the eye of the storm, it's always easier said than done. But from experience, I can tell you that embracing the pain you are going through will be your fuel and will catapult you into changing and breaking through thresholds that you've never been forced to break through.

These down, desperate, and depressed times in your life are the foundation for the greatest times in your life. Those events force you to do things you've never done. If you aren't successful and you don't have the life you want, it's because you're doing only what needs to be done. You're not putting for extra effort to reach beyond yourself.

If you want a life that you don't currently have, you have to do things that you've never done before. The change may be very uncomfortable, painful, and drastically outside your comfort zone. My advice to force that out of you, if you're not in desperate times, is to change your environment. Again, if you're going through a very depressed and catastrophic time right now, that environment alone will usually be enough to force you to take the new actions that are going to get you new results.

I'm a fan of starting small. I'm a fan of not overwhelming myself with twenty-five things I have to do tomorrow. That kind of strategy doesn't work. Trust me, I've been there. Rather, find one person who is where you want to be or at least climbing. Associate with someone who can see eye to eye with you and nurture, help, support, and encourage you.

When you meet for coffee or have lunch with that person, new seeds will be planted inside you that have never been planted before. They will eventually sprout possibility and thoughts and actions that you never thought of. As those seeds sprout, you plant seeds in the other person, and eventually other people around you. You will grow in the positive direction and start attracting other people who see things like you do, are also climbing, or are at places where you want to be. These infinite connections will start to occur in your life, and that's how the upward spiral starts.

You may currently be in a situation that you can't easily break out of. And some people closest to you may be hindering your success. I'm not saying walk away from all that you know right now. I'm saying to carve out a small amount of time to regularly engage with someone who is like-minded. It's easier now than ever to communicate with people because of the Internet. Find someone who can confirm and affirm the new thinking you desire and the new external circumstances and events in your life that you desire. One acorn can represent a forest of a thousand oak trees moving forward. Find an acorn. Do the right things with one acorn and produce a thousand-tree forest.

COMFORT VERSUS SUCCESS

Here's the deal, humans love comfort. Comfort triggers the brain that we are safe. The brain is wired for survival, to preserve the human species. When we are comfortable, the brain confirms that behavior. When we're comfortable, we know our lives aren't in danger, we know we don't have to engage the fight or flight instinct. The problem nowadays is that humans go into fight or fight mode in scenarios that aren't biologically dangerous. When fight or flight kicks in, it makes a rock-solid connection in the brain that we need to stay away from that event because it's dangerous. Fight or flight should never have kicked in, but it does because we are scared of things that have nothing to do with survival.

Comfort is poisonous to success. All the magic and success happens in discomfort. The beauty of the brain is its neuroplasticity, the more you force yourself to do uncomfortable things, the more you rewire the brain to understand that many things actually aren't anything to panic about. In time, those things eventually become normal and safe to your brain, and that is your new normal. Crossing that threshold is not easy, and that's why I tell people to start with one thing at a time and let the seeds sprout. You can be in a place where things that used to paralyze you with fear are now accomplished with ease.

Years ago when I first started in the real estate business, when I was 18 or 19 years of age, I had to talk to sellers of homes. From ads in the newspaper, I'd call the sellers to make deals. But in the beginning, I had limiting beliefs in my head, and I was scared because they were older. The thought of calling them freaked me out at first. I kept playing different scenarios in my head, and it was a very scary feeling. Sometimes when I saw a good opportunity in an ad, I wouldn't even pursue it because I was scared. I feared what could happen; I had self-conscious thoughts. Because it was all new to me, I had lots of mental hurdles to jump over.

The most comfortable thing to do was to go back to my "comfortable" life. But I really wanted to succeed, so one day I decided to pick up the phone and dial the number. I embraced the fact that I would possibly say all the wrong things and sound stupid, and some fight or flight brain activity might kick in and cause me to say the wrong things, but I made it through the first call. And guess what? The second call was easier because I made the first call. Then I made the third call. And on and on it went.

Your brain will slowly recognize that the new behavior is acceptable, it's not threatening, and it's okay. You can be comfortable even though your brain told you it's initially extremely uncomfortable.

My whole belief system changed as I made more and more intimidating calls, to the point it turned into, "Talking to older sellers is no big deal, this is what I do." I expanded my comfort zone to the next level, which was extremely crucial. Each of those small successes led to larger and larger successes.

Whether a successful billionaire, celebrity, or successful in some other area of life, that person's success can be traced back to a point where he or she chose to do the uncomfortable thing until it turned into a normal, everyday occurrence. They forced themselves into environments, circumstances, and around people where they felt extremely uncomfortable; it didn't feel like the norm. But they had to do it because their incentive was so strong and they focused on the repercussions if they didn't do it. The brain finally adjusts.

DIGESTIBLE ACTIONS

The brain releases reward chemicals in the form of endorphins, dopamine, and other chemicals and hormones when we do things that scare us or when we do things that we love. That's why I'm a firm believer in starting with the small result. Taking on an entire world in a day doesn't work; I've tried those kinds of things. I'm a fan of creating success extremely fast, and it's very possible. But breaking it down to digestible actions is the key that allows great success quickly because the brain will shoot you the new information, "That was a good result. It's okay to do the next step."

Results are extremely important. Taking on the world in a day doesn't work because you won't get a real result, which means you're going to be back to "square one" over and over again. When you plant a seed and get a small result, boom, a physiological brain connection is made. Things change not just in your mind but also in your actions. You make the next move and things change in your mind and body. Then you make the next move and things change in your mind and body. Pretty soon you're not forcing yourself to do anything because all new pathways in the brain have been developed for this new action and activity. That's the beauty of the brain; it can be completely rewired, and you can consciously rewire it into your favor to create exactly what you want in your life.

CATASTROPHIC TIMES

Consider this scenario: If something catastrophic happened on Earth and we lost all power, all vehicles were useless, houses were destroyed, all technology as we know it was gone, and Mother Earth is staring us in the face, asking how we plan to survive, what would we do? Our instincts would kick in and we would do what we have to do. We will build weather-proof shelters, start fires from scratch, hunt for and gather food from the environment, etc.

Although we have no experience in this type of primitive living, we would have to embrace the catastrophic event as it forces us across a threshold, operating on an almost super-human level, to survive. The survival instinct is embedded in us. We have no choice.

It goes back to the beautiful scenario that during catastrophic times, the positive result you won't see until you're out of it is that it forced you to open the door to a whole new level of extremely productive action. You gained new levels of understanding in life and new levels of success that you never would have known except for the extreme and catastrophic circumstances. Wherever you are, it's okay as long as you're still breathing. You are actually progressing even though you don't know it.

Most people experience failure or are unsuccessful because they're too comfortable to take the actions that create success. I think it's a tough pendulum people swing on but the reality is, most people aren't successful because they're not forced into doing what it takes. They may receive a good salary and have enough saved as a safety net to help if something bad happens. I'm not against safety nets, but if you're not forced into getting uncomfortable and doing things that you're not used to doing, you will not move up to the next level in life.

Again, extreme devastation can be a great blessing. When I look back at my financial downfall from my large entrepreneurial success prior to that, it was an enormous blessing. It was the greatest thing that happened to me in the world of success because it opened my eyes to a whole new worldview, a whole new way of operating as a person and as an entrepreneur. I'm extremely grateful it happened; I can't stress that enough.

As you climb, you'll realize there are always new thresholds to cross, and you have to continue the "rewiring" process. Some people cool off as soon as they break one or two thresholds; that is unfortunate. As you gain momentum, the climb won't feel as tough because breaking through thresholds is part of your new behavior as a whole, and it has a cumulative effect. The new circumstances and environments will start to appear. You'll see small results, and your brain will reward those results, which means there will not be as much of a fight for the new results.

You must always be trying to cross new thresholds and stay uncomfortable. The more you operate outside your comfort zone, the wider spectrum of life you're going to experience and achieve. There will come a time when the discomfort isn't nearly as strong, and you'll be *comfortable* being *uncomfortable*, knowing it is just another day in growth, and growth itself will be its own reward and incentive as you progress. It turns into an exciting upward cycle as you continue.

6

THERE IS NO "BOX"

I'm excited to talk about the "think outside the box" theory because there's actually no "box" to think outside of. Everything in this world is relative to something else—it's how humans define something. We base our perceptions on something we've already perceived. So the fact that there's even a "box" to think outside of, really doesn't make any sense if you're looking at it from a completely objective viewpoint. I've heard it said that "Normal is just a setting on your dryer."[1] It's true.

In thinking about how this person or that person is successful, we are comparing what they do or don't do in relation to how we do or don't do something. It also has to do with the lens through which we are looking. Remember, our past experiences shape how we actually view what a "normal" person is doing, and that view is far from objective.

Another person could define the exact same event or situation differently based on what they've been conditioned to believe. Part of it is beliefs, and part of it is experiences, and everything in between determines how you see the world.

IT'S ALL RELATIVE

We all know that the number of people who pursue success and actually succeed is a very small percentage of the total population. Most people follow the herd, never or seldom breaking out of the status quo. When you're pursuing success, you will be labeled weird, different, obsessive, and other unkind terms—that's how the majority defines whatever is outside of their norm. That doesn't mean pursuing success is normal or abnormal. There's no such thing, because abnormal and normal are relative to something else that someone perceives as normal or abnormal.

It all comes down to what each person chooses to think about people or situations based on their particular circumstances and experiences. Some things live on in most people's minds as more "normal" than others. But whatever you're doing, no matter what anyone says, if it's normal to you, it's freaking normal. If it's normal to you and the majority of the people around you call it weird, that's okay. Just understand that as you climb in the world of success, you'll face more and more opposition.

If normal is working 9 to 5 and doing things that make you miserable, who would ever want to be normal? Unfortunately, most people adopt this normal because they don't want to look weird and they fear uncertainty. I'm here to tell you that if you plan on succeeding in this world, plan on enduring skepticism and opposition. Naturally, thicker skin will develop as you become better at facing the opposition. Remember, if people say that what you're doing isn't normal, just realize that there's no such thing as a "universal normal."

Everyone has their own measuring stick that they use for their world, but if what you're doing works for you and it feels right, it is right. It is the norm for you. Don't let people's labels deter what you're doing; labels are only relative to their unique personal experiences.

The thread throughout this book is that each person has his or her own DNA and world experience. There are no two alike. How could you ever dream of basing anything you say or do on another human's thoughts or ideas, on what they think is right or wrong? I'm not saying to break laws or ethical borders, because we don't want to compromise our integrity, but I am saying, "You can go as far outside of the so-call 'box' that you need to." What is the box? Who defined the box? Who can say, "This is the box and what you're doing is way outside of the box"? We could have an infinite conversation about inside the box and outside the box.

Your own evolution will constantly reveal the exact calibration to the world that you have. And as you grow, your definition of the world will continually change—what was perfectly normal to you five years ago, will mostly likely be totally different today. That is healthy and part of your own personal evolution.

Again, I stress that you have to work with what your internal abilities and resources are and nurture them accordingly—regardless what people say. You have the ability to create your own life script. Too many people allow the prewritten script by certain societies in certain cultures to dictate their own life path to success.

Another important reminder: don't fall in love with other successful people and the script that they wrote for success. There is no universal code for success. You might think, *Oh well, I'm going to base my normal on ultra-successful people's normal. That will make me different. That's thinking outside the box.* Yes, you can harvest certain wisdoms and shortcuts from already-successful people, but you are comparing apples and oranges because their paths are unique and infinitely different from yours, as similar as the goal may seem.

CLAIM YOUR NORMAL

There's only one script for your life that you can play out, and it's the one that you write. Again, if you want to copy successful people and do what they've done, understand that you still have to develop your own internal ability to create your path to success. Their normal is relative to what they've experienced in life—they don't represent a universal code of success.

If what you want to do feels right internally and feels normal, claim it as your normal. Don't base your goals on someone else's viewpoint—because it's all relative. It's not right and wrong. It's just one thing relative to another.

It goes back to how we are wired. A cheetah is fast. Fast compared to what? What's slow? Slow compared to what? A rabbit's faster than a turtle, but relative to a 747 airliner, it's not. If you say someone's successful, compared to what? Compared to who? In his or her experiences, there may be many things associated with that success that you may not want. Your definition of success itself is relative to your unique experience.

Your success path can and will evolve over time, and it is healthy for it to do so. When you stand firm today and say, "I want X," you need to realize that X could drastically change over the next five to ten years, and that is totally okay because that's part of your unique experience and path through this world. This kind of evolution is what makes life interesting and beautiful. As much as you say, "In ten years I want exactly this," I believe that your desire may evolve into something different, even drastically different, and the smile on your face will be even bigger because the actual journey is part of the success you're trying to create. Don't be too rigid in your approach. The success path can be extremely beautiful—if you allow it to be.

Your unique circumstances and DNA can revolutionize whatever you thought success was. You can paint a beautiful picture of success for your life that looks nothing like any other successful person's picture on the planet. Everything is relative, and the sooner you embrace that, the sooner you will break away from the rigid constructs you have believed will create success. It's so important to understand that sticking with extreme rigidity based on someone else's principles prevents you from walking the beautiful, unique path of your own.

Some of the happiest and most successful people are the ones who stepped onto a road that had lots of uncertainty, yet understood and embraced the fact that evolution is the only way to proceed on your journey. They understood that extreme rigidity without any deviation forces a break down before getting to the true light at the end of the tunnel in the world of success.

SUCCESS IS A LIFESTYLE

Success is a lifestyle and it goes way beyond wealth and money. Obviously, when you achieve a level of financial independence, you have more choices and time, which results in alleviating a lot of life stresses. Most everyone strives to attain that level of living. The bottom line: money purchases time and freedom, and those are the two purchases I would love every person who reads this book to be able to make. The fancy cars and houses and vacations are all secondary to the those two main cash purchases (time and freedom). Time and freedom are very valuable, and the world we live in forces us to write an actual check for them.

The relativity of success is more important to understand than you may think; if you view success from someone else's play book, you will be miserable. For example, you won't consider yourself successful until you have a Ferrari—because so and so has a Ferrari. That thought alone will fire off the wrong series of brain processes that hinder you from taking the correct actions for yourself. Rigidity also hinders your progress. Your life is a totally, 100 percent unique experience to this world.

Give up the constructs that are defined by others. Define things any way *you* want. It's your world. It's your "box," and you don't have to be or think outside or inside. As long as you're operating in whatever kind of description you make of yourself, you're on your way to fulfilling your success evolution.

There is an infinite amount of space called human imagination. When you truly understand the capability of your human brain and the infinite amount of creativity and imagination it has, you can do and be anything.

The bottom line: the "box" is what the herd is thinking and saying at the time; it's a term someone thought of to generalize human thinking. Nonsense. If you want to learn more about "non-box" thinking, I encourage you to visit SuccessFromScratch.net.

ENDNOTE

1. This phrase became popular from the book written by Patsy Clairmont, *Normal Is Just a Setting on Your Dryer* (Colorado Springs, CO: Focus on the Family, 1998).

7

THE WISDOM BELT

I like to use the expression, "Wisdom is earned, not learned." Wisdom is earned from experience. There is a difference between knowledge and wisdom. I am a huge advocate of gaining new knowledge from reading books, taking courses, and learning new information, but there comes a point where only experience can teach you certain things.

When I look back at my career, I know I am where I am today because of the wisdom I gained from my successes and my failures. I actually learned much more from the downfalls and the things that went against me because it forced me to rise up. My bankruptcy was actually a "super experience"—it added a notch in my "wisdom belt."

When things go wrong and failures occur, it forces us to rise to the occasion and ask ourselves, *Why did it go wrong? Why did this happen? Why did that happen?* When we ask ourselves those questions, it forces us to think, grow, and make progress. When things are flying high and we're successful and everything seems to be going our way, we're not learning new things and being forced to break out and gain new understandings. Knowledge only goes so far, and I feel like when you are going through your failures and your negative situations, you should understand that every single one of them is putting a notch in your wisdom belt.

The more notches you have—aka the more failures you have—the better you can receive the opportunities coming to you in the present and in the future, because you have a belt of experience. You will think, *Oh in this case, this is what I did and it didn't work, so I'm going to do it another way next time.* It forces a faster evolution to success.

Knowledge is information that can be very valuable and drastically enhance your ability to create success; wisdom comes from taking action and seeing things as more than theory. At the end of the day, knowledge and facts are great to read and talk about, but when put into action, they are ingrained deeply within. As you journey on and new situations come up, your mind and body will react based on your knowledge.

It seems that many older people seem to have a lot more wisdom. Why is that? Because they've had more experiences. Over the years they faced diverse situations in the world and, in general, found their own way and slowly evolved from trial and error. Most older people have many notches in their belts. Now they know that when certain things happen, they respond correctly, because they've been through it before. You have to go through things to earn wisdom.

When you go through extremely catastrophic or traumatic events, you can extract years or even decades of wisdom from that one experience. The larger and more catastrophic the events you go through, the wiser you become. Those experiences *force* your mind and consciousness to flex to places it never would have without the extreme events.

Creating success is a combination of gaining the right knowledge, exposing yourself to new experiences, and then earning wisdom from both. Balancing knowledge and experiences is important. You have to bring in new information while acting on opportunities—sometimes stumbling and making mistakes along the way—then you are truly having it ingrained inside, which allows you to be better, more nimble, and react the right way to things moving forward.

At the end of the day, you want wisdom and experience to lead you to a deeper yet higher level.

Unexpected situations and issues and uncertainties will happen in life, but the more experience you have, the better you will react and handle those experiences. Whatever negative situations you have gone through, or are going through currently, are all part of putting the right notches in your wisdom belt to shape who you will truly become. It's hard to see as you go through it, but it's imperative to realize you're being positively shaped for a great future.

Every negative circumstance and failure has value, and those negative circumstances and failures can't be taught to you from a book. Someone can theorize about failure and explain everything that they've been through, but you'll never actually internalize it or fully understand it until you've been through it yourself. Once you've been through it, you will have the wisdom to navigate the dark waters in the future. All the negative experiences and all the failures can definitely be used to your advantage, touching on the lens and viewpoint discussed previously.

YOUR UNIQUE INTERPRETATION

Whatever you experience and whatever lessons you learn are interpreted uniquely by you. Failures produce more than any success because when you are succeeding, there is less likelihood or desire to self-reflect, which is important. Self-reflection is very important on the journey to succeeding and growing. But when you're constantly succeeding, you have less incentive to self-reflect because you think you're doing everything correctly. When you're failing and running into road blocks and brick walls and things aren't going your way, you will inevitably take a step back and ask, *What am I doing wrong? How can I improve? How can I progress? How can I change things?* I'm a firm believer in embracing major obstacles in order to succeed—obstacles develop your wisdom muscles.

For example, a major catastrophic event that is felt worldwide will be interpreted differently by each human on the planet because of each person's unique brain architecture. Even if people have very similar points of view, there are still micro-differences in their perception of the event. These differences can be developed into your own unique approach, your own unique wisdom and knowledge about how to handle situations in front of you. When a "brick wall" is presented to you, and the same "brick wall" is presented to someone else, your inner wisdom will spark solutions. Gaining and acting on your own wisdom supersedes any type of intelligence or knowledge that can be learned from a book. It's a true-life experience being internalized and then intertwined with your unique DNA and brain structure.

Developing wisdom from a negative life experience is partially a choice. Part of it is going to happen regardless, but the wiser you are, the more you understand that obstacles in life are part of the sculpting of your unique wisdom. That wisdom will carry over and grow throughout your life.

Unforeseen external forces and situations will happen regardless of our degree or race or financial status. We have no control over certain external forces in our lives, but where we do have control is morphing those external forces, failures, negativities, pessimistic people, obstacles, etc. into things we can develop for our benefit. We must take a step back and look at why it happened, how it happened, and develop our wisdom so that we have a wider point of view, a greater degree of perception to handle these situations moving forward. As you progress through your life and mature as someone who succeeds, you'll realize that every event, especially the negative ones, is designed to design you.

WHAT'S NEXT?

Since I've had the privilege of helping people around the world succeed through my various teaching methods, I have noticed that many people get stuck in a "What should I do next?" mindset. They have the "how to" steps in place, but want me to tell them the next step and the next step. That's when I differentiate wisdom and knowledge to them: *wisdom* is understanding that wisdom can be developed from knowledge and experiences; *knowledge* is external and has to be continually absorbed.

Wisdom comes from inside; when you take action with knowledge, your "wisdom muscle" will develop. That's a very important aspect of being successful, otherwise you will be stuck in the "What do I do next" mindset, needing your hand held on the journey to success, which will never get you there.

Some people get stuck in that mindset because they worry about obstacles so obsessively that they never take action. They think, *"Let me read more, understand more, ask my mentor more,"* to the point where every micro situation is being managed by some other form of knowledge and they never actually develop the skill of wisdom itself. Wisdom involves taking action—and getting punched in the face sometimes.

Self-reliance is also a skill that can be developed. Some people have natural inclinations to be independent, but most must develop the skill, which is one of the most important skills on your journey to success. Self-reliance means not relying on someone telling you what to do next.

Asking questions and curiosity is extremely healthy and imperative on your journey; but know that as you make progress, the fact of facing uncertainty remains constant. Questions will arise about the next step, but you have to be able to maneuver into things that are uncertain, because 100 percent certainty doesn't exist in the world of succeeding.

In fact, the constant need for 100 percent certainty will be the ultimate hindrance to your success.

Some people are almost obsessed with knowing what happens next because it makes them feel more comfortable than running into a brick wall. Listen, brick walls teach you more than any "million-dollar" knowledge from the greatest book in the world. The brick wall interacts directly with your unique mind and body, and that combination produces the ability to proceed, even without knowing all the answers. You will realize that you have the ability to solve problems in general, regardless what the problem may be.

PROBLEM-SOLVING SKILL SET

It's important to understand that there are an infinite multitude of problems that will arise on your journey to success. By developing the "problem-solving skill," you will understand that when new problems appear, you have a universal problem-solving skill set already in place. You will think, *Okay, This is something beyond my control and I've never seen before and don't even fully understand, but I know I have the problem-solving muscle inside me. I will figure it out and use my unique abilities to not only learn from the new challenge, but to also get through it successfully, because my problem-solving skill set has been developed over time.*

The ultimate power within yourself is when you can think that with confidence and then take action to tackle the issue head-on. The problem-solving skill can be fully developed regardless of who you are and where you come from. In fact, all of the principles presented in this book are worthy of developing. It's just a matter of how serious you are to proceed and take action to develop the principles in your life.

Science has proven that the more senses we activate, the better we are at learning. For example, you can read a book on how to solve a problem, but going out and physically experiencing the problem and using your mind and all your senses to solve the problem will lock in that structure of wisdom, allowing you to proceed much further and faster. And you won't have to ask someone, "What should I do next?" every time you turn a corner.

A caution: The Internet is full of success teachers and success talk and how to become successful. But because each person is unique, what makes one person successful may not make another person successful. The issue I have with many success teachers is that they put forth a universal force and one universal set of actions that will supposedly bring you success. I firmly believe that *the key to success* is developing your own self-awareness, and then developing your own path to success.

You have to tap into yourself and understand what you're able to do, and what you're not able to do. You can't succeed when trying to do something that your abilities don't match. Your journey to succeed is based on where you are, what you can develop internally, and then how you can take action and move forward from where you are. Every person has their own path. Every person has a different way of succeeding. What one person does to succeed could be the polar opposite of what another person does to succeed— that's the beauty of this world.

Failures are the most important teachers; failures reveal your internal world 100 percent more than successes do. I want to go back to the point of how successes prevent self-reflect. Failures are the ultimate equalizers that open your eyes and say, "Hey, you're doing this wrong," or, "Hey, your perspective is incorrect, you need to change your viewpoint in order to move forward." Those roadblocks are absolutely mandatory because they reveal what needs to be done to move ahead.

I've heard it said often that "What got you here, won't get you there," and I try to live by that fact because it's true. What got you to this exact point in success is phenomenal, but if you want to get to a further point, you may have to do things completely differently. It may be 180-degrees different from your initial steps to get to that point, but that's totally okay because that's part of the progression of succeeding.

8

MOST EVENTS ARE NEUTRAL

Our reaction to events—situations, problems, circumstances—will make or break our success. Most events are neutral, not requiring an immediate outburst of positive or negative reaction. But many times we haven't developed emotional maturity and we react from emotion rather than logic. When it comes to succeeding, unchecked emotions can drastically sabotage our chances to succeed. Emotions remove logical thought and we make decisions based on temporary feelings.

Many times throughout my entrepreneurial career, I did things based on pure emotion that I wouldn't dream of doing today. I reacted with zero logic. For example, when I was landlording my properties, there were tenants who wouldn't pay their rent and would do things that really irritated me. So I called them, threatened them, and yelled at them based on pure, out-of-control emotion. In turn, my attitude forced them to be defensive and retaliate against me—and problems spiraled. After I totally lost my temper one day with a tenant who owed me three months' rent, she got defensive and actually sabotaged the property by causing the basement sewer drain to flood, which destroyed some of her own things—then she sued me for three times what they were worth. Long story short, we went to court, and after month and months of turmoil, attorney fees, and gut-wrenching stress, she won.

If I could go back in time with the wisdom and knowledge that I gained over the years, I would respond and react intelligently to the situation. I would perhaps send her a letter and offer something like, "I will wipe clean your three late rent payments if you move out before next Friday." I would use a completely different kind of strategy.

My emotions got the best of me. If I would have been more entrepreneurially mature, something like that never would have happened. These days I take a deep breath, zoom out and look at the scenario as neutral, and then handle it logically and calmly. I am objective and understanding of all the actual facts, instead of my own emotionally charged perception of the facts. Many times I need to swallow my pride and the outcome is extremely favorable.

Another example of being young in age and in emotional maturity is when I took on a building inspector at one of my properties. I said things I shouldn't have said to him and soon after, I was clobbered with all kinds of citations and work orders and was targeted for many little things that could have been easily remedied. I had to go to court to defend myself because of property code violations. I allowed my ego to rule and my emotional outburst drastically turned a neutral event into a major problem.

Looking back, at the time, I resented his egotistical attitude and became overly defensive. I realize now that there are many personalities in the world and I need to adjust my reactions to accommodate each one—without compromising my integrity or sense of self. It would have been better to cater to his superiority complex—stroke his ego, agree with him (within reason), smile, and tell him he was correct. Then there would have been no need to retaliate or defend himself because I didn't attack him.

That event was neutral. He was a building inspector doing his job. I was a property owner. We must take the high road, have higher thoughts, and realize that the best result will be attained if we put our egos aside, swallow our pride, and understand that this is a natural and neutral scenario. Our reactions determine whether it turns out positively or negatively.

LESSONS LEARNED

I'm not asking you to compromise your convictions and values. There is a line you have to draw; but in most situations (especially on the path to success), you don't need to cross ethical or convictional borders within yourself to get what you want. You just have to understand that every scenario is neutral, and if you use intelligence over emotion, and develop a higher mind of looking at things, you will get much further, much faster, with much less resistance.

This is one of the greater lessons I've learned throughout the successes and great failures of my life. If it seems that negative scenarios are coming at you from every angle and you feel defensive, they may be the result of the many emotional and ego-defensive micro decisions you've made over time. Based on my examples, you can most likely see that various battles started out as neutral events—not positive or negative. The initial event was an everyday occurrence, but because emotions went wild, it turned into a battle. Rather, we must learn to react intelligently and leave emotions out of it.

This is much easier said than done because we are emotional creatures. We operate on emotion much of the time. But on your climb to success, you have to realize that there is strategy, and strategy trumps effort. The more strategic you are, the more you develop your strategic muscles. You will naturally start reacting with intelligence and strategy over emotion and ego. That fact is imperative to grasp. You have to look at events and facts with complete objectivity; the more you do that, the more you will make correct decisions. The "fight or flight" mindset also tosses out the window logical thought, and the results from that can have damaging effects on progress.

Nobody's perfect, but controlling your emotions is something you should work on developing. You should take a deep breath before you react and try to look at things as objectively as possible. Look at the factors at play, and look at the result you want. Then use a higher mind to make decisions throughout this neutral circumstance that could go one way or another. It's your choice which way it goes.

Life throws you certain curveballs that are just flat-out negative. Not every event is neutral. There are devastating wars, diseases, loss of loved ones, etc. There are certain things in the world that aren't neutral, but most are. Objectivity gives you the intelligence to make the best possible decisions. Over time, you'll get better and better at being objective.

A CONSCIOUS EFFORT

Most changes in your life start out as conscious acts. If you want to lose weight, you consciously change your diet and start to exercise. That's not always easy. You have to consciously think about how to act in the given situations that you're trying to change. As we do things over and over, our physiology starts to turn our new behaviors into muscle memory. It turns into automation. The brain enjoys shortcuts, and if it can recognize consistent patterns, it will actually move that action to a whole other part of the brain that doesn't take as much conscious effort. It moves to a more automated section of the brain so you can focus your conscious mind on something new.

It's kind of like learning how to ride a bike. When you first get on the bike as a child, you think about all the moving parts and about the movement of your legs. You may think, *I might fall!* You think about the handlebars, tires, brakes, and the bell. You think about all these micro events simultaneously and very consciously; but after you ride around the block a few times, your brain actually takes this entire operation of riding a bike and moves it to another part of your brain because it computes as "Check, we got this. We're going to move that to the fast highways of neuron connections where the operation of the bike flows automatically." We don't think about it consciously anymore.

Now when you ride a bike, you can think about the weather, a basketball game, or your success journey—you have to put zero conscious thought into the actual riding. This change, among others that we're talking about, applies to your ability to do this with your mind, body, and nervous system.

Reaction to events is very important and we definitely cannot take this aspect of success lightly. Reaction to events in our lives make or break our quality of life, because we can't control external circumstances much of the time—but we *can* control our reactions. Our quality of life is strongly correlated to how we react to problems, situations, and circumstances. And how we react allows us to learn, gain wisdom, and gain more objectivity so that we can proceed with a higher mind, which allows us to gain our success faster.

9

THE TIME RESOURCE

All people have the same twenty-four hours in every day. In all reality, time is the universal equalizer of all commodities. It's the universal resource. We can't point fingers and declare, "Well, they have this much time and I only have this much." Some people use their time resource wisely, and some people waste it.

Successful people look at time as a strategic resource. Each minute is significant in their world; they use each one wisely. I really want to dive into this topic because traditional success gurus and teachers talk about how you have to wake up early, stay up late, and do business, business, business all day, every day. You don't.

If your time management is laser focused, you can accomplish power moves in a fraction of the time it would take someone else. The reason is because many people hustle, but they don't strategically and smartly hustle. Most people I know who are "trying" to become successful are frustrated that things aren't going anywhere, and this is a major reason why they aren't moving forward.

For example, when I started my education company—teaching real estate—I was already running my successful real estate business, yet I also wanted to write a book and teach people online how to do what I do in real estate. I knew how time consuming all that would be and that the learning curve would be substantial. I also knew that time management was crucial because my real estate business couldn't be ignored, nor did I want to cut into spending quality time with my beloved family.

SIGNIFICANT SHORTCUTS

Back in the early days when I knew I wanted to teach my real estate entrepreneurship skills to the world, I hired a coach. I hired someone who knew how to write books successfully and get a message heard worldwide. I purchased years of his mistakes upfront. That was unbelievably important. It allowed me to cut years of learning curves off my life, which was strategic. Most people would say, "I can figure this one out," and then spend months or years spinning their wheels, going nowhere. I'm not knocking the hands-on approach, because I still learn that way a lot of the time. But over the years as I've matured as an entrepreneur, I've realized that there are many shortcuts, and I'm willing to take every single one. Don't ever let anybody tell you that shortcuts are unacceptable or not ethical. Your hands-on learning, combined with shortcuts, is how you can grow fast.

Look at a book, coach, or course like buying compounded hours. Purchasing people's mistakes upfront is a significant, solid shortcut. Find someone who's where you want to be, and purchase all of their mistakes, learning lessons, and trials upfront through coaching, online training, courses, or books. That's always a great place to start. As you evolve and start taking your own action, you will quickly realize that there are easier ways to systemize things and make processes that replace your own constant action. This is something I learned quickly through my coach and through my own trial and error. Start focusing on optimizing all of your time because it's finite; once it's gone, it's gone.

I am obsessed with finding shortcuts and "hacks" to allow me to have free time. I have compounded hours packed into one hour. How about compounded weeks packed into days? What about compounded years packed into a month? This concept actually grew into a slight obsession of mine, because I know how valuable time is. As I look back over my life, I can't believe how fast those years disappeared. You may be feeling the same way. Time freaking flies. If you have kids, you see how quickly they grow up. If I can pack an extended period of time into a shorter time, I'm going to do that like clockwork (pardon that cheesy pun).

Life is too short to make every possible mistake to get to wherever you want to go. Rather, you can execute with laser-targeted precision and cut your learning curve by having outsiders help you, seeking advice from a mentor, or by purchasing learning materials that compact someone else's time and mistakes so you can bypass all of them.

No doubt you have heard or read of two people starting out from scratch, and one person becomes very successful and the other doesn't. Maybe that happened to you. I don't believe in the philosophy that says, "Successful people were born under the right star" and there's some supernatural force that allowed them to be successful. No. I believe successful people used their time in the most strategic way possible. You had the same twenty-four hours they did. They just used those twenty-four hours as strategically as possible; they compacted years and years of lessons from other people into shorter amounts of time, so they could get to where they are faster.

Fortunately, this day and age allows us to propel very quickly. Success has a lower barrier to entry than it did one hundred years ago. This is great for you, but it does create the new herd, as mentioned previously. Although you have to separate yourself from them, you don't need mountains of time to get where you want to go. The key is to be strategic with the time that you do have.

TIME IS THE EQUALIZER

One of the most used excuses I hear from people is that they don't have time to create the life they have wanted for decades and decades for themselves and their family. They don't have time? I don't buy it. On the other hand, I receive emails from people who write, "Hey Nick, just for all those people who say they don't have time, here's me holding a check for $10,000. I did this deal, and I have three kids who are all involved in sports. I'm married. I work 40 hours a week, and have a part-time job. And I still had time to do this deal to help change my life."

Time is the equalizer. You can't point at someone and say they have time and I don't. You either use it wisely, or you get nowhere. Time is just like money—live below your means and invest the difference. Some people can live more below their means and have a bigger difference to invest. Even if it's a very small difference, take that difference of time and employ it for your growth.

Some people have more physical time than others, but everyone has the ability to carve out time for their actual priorities. People who say they don't have time are really telling me that it's not a true priority. People make time for priorities. If you don't strategize and make the time to pursue your success, then succeeding isn't really a priority. There's always one thing you can cut out to get that sliver of time to spend on your growth. From there, it will build upon itself, but it starts with one small sliver. Then it compounds and exponentially grows. Period, it's not debatable.

If success is a true priority, not just wishful thinking or something you hope to attain someday, time will be there. The reality is most people hope to be successful, wish to be successful, and think it's going to somehow knock on their door. The reality is that using time wisely, as limited as it may be, can and will compound in your favor if you are strategic about using it to become successful.

Time can be on your side or against you based on your own perception and priority of time. How you prioritize time will make or break your success—or failure. *What your physical reality is tomorrow drastically depends on what you do with your perception of time today.*

Time will compound if you are strategic in the beginning with the sliver of it that you have. As time, freedom, and your economic scenario grows, more and more of it will be available. The key is to continue to engage in the activities that compound massive amounts of time into the shortest amount of time.

Some people seem to have lots of time and other people seem to always be running out of time. Both types of people need to see time the right way. It's all about what you do with the time that you do have. There are plenty of stories told about people who inherit millions of dollars and lose it quickly because they don't have the wealth mindset and aren't strategic in their handling of the money. Then there are people with little to zero money who are strategic with what they have, and go on to make millions of dollars in wealth.

Time is the same type of resource. What are you doing with your hours and minutes and seconds? Managing the time you have will make the difference for you. Focus on your timing and execute wisely.

10

COMPARISON IS POISON

When on the road to success, don't look at other people's success. If you think you need to do this or that because he or she did it and became successful, your focus is wrong. All that kind of thinking does is cloud the only thing that matters—your internal awareness of yourself and the actions that you take accordingly. There's absolutely no reason to compare your journey to success with someone else's. You need to be in your own lane and be yourself. You have a unique skill set and a unique DNA structure. You were designed with special abilities, inclinations, desires, knowledge base, etc. That's the beauty of this world—and of you.

Yes, you can learn lifetimes worth of shortcuts and tweaks to get you to success, but if you're constantly comparing your journey to other people's, it can devastate your progress. If you are so focused on what they're doing, you won't be focusing on your unique way of doing things, you'll lose sight of where you stand in your own journey. I'm not saying you shouldn't take some wisdom from successful people and model some of their behaviors and actions, but it's not the "be all, end all" to success.

Realize that your mental energy is a *finite* resource. If you're constantly putting your energy into what other people are doing, you're wasting energy—use your energy toward focusing on your own journey.

Harvest what you can from other people's successes, then internalize it to operate from your unique standpoint and approach. That's the most important lesson that you can take away from looking at other people's success.

When I first started, I knew I wanted to dominate the world as a successful real estate entrepreneur and investor. I made a lot of progress quickly, but I also remember seeing other people who had more buildings and were making more deals than I was at the time. I would try to pick apart what they were doing, and sometimes I was envious of their positions. Envy can deplete finite energy. Envy is a bandwidth hog in the brain. I firmly believe that envy can tie up major mental bandwidth. That's a serious problem; we need as much bandwidth as possible to make our unique dent in the world.

Early on I would think, *So-and-so is doing that, why can't I? Why can so-and-so make so many deals per month and I can't? What is he doing?* Envy was tying up mental bandwidths that I could have been using to take actions for my own growth; instead, I was heavily focused on other people's growth, and that's not healthy. Dipping into our mental resources to focus on other people and what they're doing prevents us from accomplishing our goals. We need to use energy toward developing our own abilities. Others have different abilities and different environments that nurtured completely different abilities that allowed them to have their success.

For example: You may know a couple who has an extremely happy marriage, and you think if you what they do, you and your spouse will have a happy marriage too. Although there are common ways to make relationships work, the bottom line is there are two unique people doing their own thing that works for them as a couple. Each couple has their own internal structure and internal abilities and disabilities to where they operate at the optimal way with what they know.

Back to your journey to success, maybe you will have to work harder or less hard—you have to uncover the internal resource that's unique to you. Don't lose track of looking inside yourself. I'm a firm believer that *looking inside yourself and developing your wisdom and your own intuition is the ultimate path to success.* The more you focus on others, the less time, energy, effort, and resources you have to put into accomplishing your goals.

I believe our brains are wired to compare and even helped humans survive thousands of years ago. Primitives most likely compared size and speed and shelters and food gathering skills—and most likely mimicked the better way of doing things.

We have a tendency to look at the upsides of others and the downsides of ourselves. When we compare, we usually see the weaker side of ourselves in certain areas. It seems to me that human-to-human comparison is not truly apples-to-apples; there are infinite amounts of different brain connections. Even if we look similar from the outside, each human is different in infinite ways, but we can learn from them—then make our own orange juice.

On the flip side, if you compare yourself to people less successful than you are, that comparison will also hinder your progress. If you feel superior, your ego will develop to a point where it won't question your actions. You won't be forced to grow because you think you're above all that. Comparing yourself to others more successful or less successful can poison and delay your journey. To read about how I fell into the comparison trap, visit SuccessFrom-Scratch.net.

11

ECONOMIC EVOLUTION

Darwin's theory of evolution maintains that the most fit of a species will survive—survival of the fittest. So how does that apply to your success? An "economic evolution" is the preservation of *you*, the preservation of your business. The economy represents nature, and the business that is the most fit will survive. You must learn how to adapt and evolve in reaction to the economy and the local, regional, or even national and worldwide business environments.

My philosophy: If things are booming, great. If things are not booming, great. I will respond accordingly. A favorite expression: "When the winds change, you have to adjust your sails." I don't care if the winds are blowing west, east, north, or south. What I *do* care about is my strategy to structure my sails to use the winds to my advantage. There may be a lot of "opposing winds" (opposition to your agenda) that can actually be used to propel you if you learn to be a master sailor and navigate yourself away from where you don't want to go. It's imperative to understand that you are in control.

Another favorite expression: "A calm sea never produced a great sailor." If every time you hop into the boat and the sea is perfectly calm, you won't be stretched to the point where you must develop the skill of navigating in rough waters.

CHOOSE YOUR ENVIRONMENT

Another part of economic evolution and survival is to go where your agenda is nurtured. Again using the nature analogy (species preservation), you must consistently choose environments that confirm your success agenda. Yes, there are environments we can't control, but most often you can choose to live and work in environments that nurture your preservation and growth as a person, business, and climber on the ladder to success.

While on the climb, stay away from people who oppose your agenda and seek out people who are supporting, nurturing, optimistic, and are bridge-builders who can make things easier for you—while at the same time you know you can handle the rough seas if they appear.

This isn't simple-minded stuff. It is important to understand the duality of the concept presented in this chapter. The economy, or your industry, doesn't care about you specifically. More now than ever, with the number of people in the world trying to succeed and make things happen, you are in a "survival of the fittest" environment—I'm trying my best to get you freaking fit.

Everyone can talk about resilience in tough economic times. But I'm talking about helping you develop higher thinking and a higher perception than all the others. There's a new herd out there, and the concepts in this book, when put into action, will stand you head and shoulders above the crowd.

One law of success is firm: adapters always win. I'm not telling you to let the wind blow you wherever, and you have to adapt to every breeze. No, I'm saying the opposite. You must be smart about adaptation. Evolvers, innovators, and adapters win in nature, and they win in the economy.

If you make necessary adjustments in your journey, your activities and innovations are rewarded, your progress advance, and you become more and more successful on an exponential basis. You will be light years ahead of any competitors. In fact, I don't even like using the word "competitors" because you are so laser focused in your own lane that you're not looking around to view competition because it doesn't matter. Your focus needs to remain on staying strong, seeing the horizon, and planning how to adapt and evolve to get there. Okay? That's what matters.

When I look back at my bankruptcy and a few other major events that drastically stretched my "adversity muscles," I think how much my problem-solving skills were developed. That's what's important. Whatever issues I face now, I am confident each one can be solved. Through my own personal evolution, I have learned to adapt and thrive, not just survive.

Economic evolution presents a dual scenario: the economy doesn't care about you and you need to adopt, evolve, and innovate in an environment where your preservation and growth is nurtured and rewarded. When you can embrace that dualism in the economic evolutionary environment, you can put yourself in a "cruise control" growth mode in your own lane, not focusing on anything other than your own journey ahead.

Your higher agenda for success is what matters most.

12

THE DEFAULT CYCLE

The default cycle is something I figured out early on in my career, on my climb to success. I noticed a roller coaster-like effect from the ups and downs of business life. When I started producing real results, like receiving a large check from a deal, I was totally hyped. But then I cooled off and my ego got in the way. Because things were smooth sailing, I became cocky. I took a backseat, relaxed, and overrewarded myself.

It's good to reward yourself when you create success and results, but don't overreward yourself, especially in the beginning when you're really trying to grow. Growth years are critical. It's when a lot of momentum can take place. You don't want to take an ounce of it for granted—like I did.

MANAGING SUCCESS

Many people take success for granted, especially when they don't know how to manage success. We talked about money management and time management, but what about results and success management? Think about that for a minute. When you start accomplishing what you set out to do, things you've never done before, how do you manage the results? That's the problem. I cooled off because I didn't know how to manage the results. The roller coaster ride goes up and down—up with success and down with the cooling off from achieving results. Sometimes the ride goes down so far that you get desperate and are forced to take actions to produce results. Then you climb back up, and the cycle continues.

I call it the "default cycle" because between the downs and ups, you revert to the mean—the average. That's not a good place to be because you're never actually climbing and growing long term. There are little climbs and then little falls; you're not going anywhere. If you really want to make the long-term climb to reach your life's dreams and goals, don't cool off. Keep stretching forward and managing your results.

I really understood the default cycle when I declared bankruptcy. I realized that I couldn't take anything for granted. It's so true that no one knows what they have till it's gone. That's a law of human nature. As I saw results and progress in the early days, I would slowly see it go away because I overrewarded myself and didn't manage my progress and results. I didn't have the experience to manage pretty significant results at such a young age.

I reverted to average. As I "zoomed out" and viewed myself and pondered my prior successes and failures, I saw that I wasn't advancing. I not only saw this stagnation in myself, I also saw it in my family, friends, acquaintances, and people learning from me how to create success. The default cycle is a place where there is no consistent growth.

Auditing yourself is okay, even encouraged. Look back at when you climbed and when you cooled off. Notice the events that took place before the highs and lows. You may right now be realizing that you've done this. You've been miserable. Your boss just destroyed you at work. Friday was the worst day of your life and you went home and thought, *I'm doing something about this right now. I'm taking massive action. I'm going to create my own success, develop my own destiny, grow, and finally make progress."* Then on Monday you received a few good results and you're up again—thinking things aren't that bad and you revert to average, to the status quo. When you know how to manage and commit to your true desires, you will make progress.

It comes down to self-awareness—being aware of what is important to you, and looking at your past and dissecting it so you can laser-target a freight train moving forward. You have to identify your own default cycle. Whatever that looks like. Everyone's default cycle looks a little different, but the process is universal.

Taking things for granted and getting comfortable poisons your success and impedes your progress. Comfort is the aversion of success. All great success comes from breaking through painful and uncomfortable thresholds. Let me tell you something, going back to the default cycle, there's a threshold at the top of the highs that you have to cross. The problem with the default cycle is that it scrapes on the edge of that upper threshold and then you start cooling off before true success and growth is gained.

Being comfortable, taking your results for granted, and not managing your results properly will poison your climb to success because it doesn't allow you to break through the miscellaneous thresholds holding you back. You don't want to revert to average because that is stagnation, which opposes your success and growth.

PLANNING AHEAD

Most people don't know to manage the ups when they get there because they've never been at the top curve of success. You need to visualize your success, put it on paper what you expect. Then when you break through that top threshold with the right effort, it won't seem so daunting. You have to be able to consistently handle the ups so you can stay up there, breaking through each new scenario.

Because many people who create success from scratch are experiencing success for the first time, it is so easy for them to fall into a default cycle after the first few positive results. A "scarcity mindset" is one key strategy I've used to keep moving forward. It forces me to keep thinking about how much more I have to learn, how much more growth is yet to be attained. Thinking that I don't know when certain doors will close makes me want to take action. Resources may be abundant now but with a scarcity mindset, I realize that I must plan ahead for when resources may not be as plentiful.

When you know that tomorrow is not guaranteed and your current success doesn't automatically guarantee future success, you use those facts to gain momentum to break through the thresholds you need for growth. You're only as good as your last result. Stay *un*comfortable.

The journey of climbing is the fun part of the whole process and it's easy to get sidetracked at the top. But know that the default cycle is vicious and dangerous. It has taken me down in the past. It has taken many people down in the past. I've seen it. But the scarcity psychology will serve you well. Success is only temporary if you don't make a conscious effort to move forward toward the next success, growing into the next uncomfortable step to cross a new threshold. When you are able to recognize the default cycle in your life, you'll know how to avoid it. It's one of those things you don't know how to correct until you see it. Self-awareness is extremely important. You can't change what you don't know is happening.

CONTINUOUS MOVEMENT

What you did to get where you are currently is not permanent. Continued success requires movement. Success loves people who are moving and evolving and adapting and operating out of a sense of scarcity. I'm not saying to produce a crazy sense of fake scarcity where you're always thinking, *I'm going to starve tomorrow if I don't improve.* No, that's not a healthy or productive mindset. Just understand that what you did yesterday to get you to today could be completely different tomorrow. You have to stay fresh. Understand that constant progress is required for constant success.

Success is constant threshold breaking and being uncomfortable. All the things you're uncomfortable doing today may have produced significant results, but that doesn't mean they will produce significant results tomorrow, a week from now, or anytime in the future. In ten years, you may look back and realize that what you're doing right now isn't even close to what you're currently doing to produce results to get to a higher level.

Lack of innovation, change, and evolution will cause your progress to stop or even regress.

Always take every opportunity to keep momentum going forward. Recognize the momentum that you created and execute like a maniac, even if money is pouring into your bank account, even if you're climbing your success ladder in ways you cannot even imagine—do not take anything for granted because momentum is the road to success. If you leverage it properly, it can carry you into the progress and success zone for decades, or even a lifetime

The right momentum can break through multiple thresholds in a short period of time. You will be able to feel it in your bones when things are happening and going in the right direction. The problem some people have is when there is momentum, they just sit still and let it take them for a while. Momentum can carry people a long way, but the word "momentum" includes the word "moment"—and the length of a moment can vary.

Believe me, the tidal wave will eventually crash. But if you made the right decisions and executed them when on top of the momentum, and really got uncomfortable and broke through thresholds, and recognized the signature moments of your life, you will continue to be propelled into a lifetime of success. It does go back to the old saying, "Strike while the iron is hot." It doesn't stay hot forever. What will you do when signature moments come your way?

13

MONETIZING YOUR PASSION IS DANGEROUS

Let's address the very popular advice of today, "Find your passion and make a living from it." There are plenty of examples where that advice has been successful. But it's not a universal success principle. You have to understand entrepreneurship, the default cycle, the way economics changes things, and you have to be self-aware. Yes you can be passionate, but I believe that your passion will evolve as you start to understand success. What you end up becoming passionate about and making a beautiful living from could look completely different from what you're thinking right now.

Part of this modern-day advice makes complete sense, and I think you should embrace the idea of making sure you love what you're doing, otherwise life is a grind and your dream turns into something you dread.

My advice to you is to understand success, entrepreneurship, progress, your mindset, and your internal world, and a new passion will be revealed. Or it may be the passion you're thinking about right now—something you love to do. I'm also saying it could evolve in a direction that you don't even know exists yet, because you may have a very primitive and immature mindset about what passion is in the world of success and entrepreneurship.

FREEDOM IS YOUR PASSION

It's best to start with the thought that *freedom is your passion* because at the end of the day, life is too short not to be free. At some level, I think everyone has a passion for freedom in their lives. You want to able to make choices, to have time with your family, to do the things you love to do. That's the ultimate transcended passion that everyone is striving for. Looking more toward that as the end goal, the passion activity you love could evolve in directions that you don't know exist yet. Then passion will explode exponentially as you start experiencing wins and successes. You only know what you know at the present moment, and things are going to evolve in ways that months or years down the road, what you once were passionate about could look completely different.

Expose yourself to new ideas and experiences, keeping the higher goal of freedom as the ultimate passion. Then everything will start to materialize in its own way.

I encourage you to make freedom your passion because too many people think they can say, "Hey, I love to play video games. I want to make a living off of that." That is not very realistic for the majority of people. Yet there may be a few who have loved video games so much that they started a membership website or wrote a best-selling book and monetized their passion.

Although this advice is being touted a lot lately, I disagree that tunnel vision regarding your passion and making money will pay off in the long run. You must have a wider perspective of your passion, the world, economics, industry changes, resources, etc. Intentionally exposing yourself to a healthy variety of externalities could evolve you in directions that will coincide with your passion and the combination will be even more exciting and lucrative. There are parts of the recipe of success that involve your passion, but that is *not* the *only* ingredient.

Having an overall passion to create *freedom* allows your more specific passion to evolve into something you may not have thought possible, something not in your current mental agenda. That's okay. Much of what I do today, if someone said ten years ago I'd be doing it, I wouldn't believe them. In fact, I'm doing things right now that were not even in my plans six months ago. I choose to expose myself to all kinds of environments, scenarios, and people. I continue to be open to exploring a variety of opportunities that although it may not be my passion now and I don't know that it even exists in the universe, a year from now I could be heavily focused on it!

Following one person's advice exclusively limits your conscious mind. Stay open to an evolution of passion, understand progress, understand success principles, understand the changes in industries and economies. Understanding success in general rather than focusing totally on one passion will very likely take you to places and heights that will blow your imagination wide open!

14

THE DIAMOND PROCESS

Creating success from scratch is hard. Success from scratch brings pressure. Diamonds, as I'm sure you know, are produced from massive amounts of pressure. Likewise, your greatest creativity, thoughts, and evolution of your consciousness can happen in times of significant pressure. These times hit you so hard and the pain is so deep you can't even stand it. It's not always easy, but if you embrace the pressure, you may break through to an unknown but wonderful place of revelation.

I've felt pressure many times during my life. I can tell you that the benefits are much clearer looking back than while you're being pressured. During those quick evolution times, my consciousness changed. My degree of perception expanded from the pressure and "diamond thoughts" or "diamond creativity" emerged. I thought of things I never would have if I didn't have the pressure, pain, and struggle of knowing I had to start from scratch.

Some people work well, even better, under pressure. Pressure produces a certain thought-flow process and creativity that actually enhances the effort and outcome. Hormones in your brain are released and actions and beliefs can change. A lot of pressure can quickly shatter old, unnecessary beliefs. Devastating scenarios—which lead to massive pressure, which lead to diamond thoughts—can shortcut negativity and produce the positive.

Classic rags-to-riches success stories originate from a certain mindset and thought process that produce diamond thoughts. These people embraced the high pressures of their rags circumstances and produced diamond thoughts, diamond creativity, and diamond evolution. What may have taken two years to learn, happens much faster.

As far as my own diamond thoughts and creativity episodes, I experienced it many times during and after my bankruptcy. Thoughts and ideas emerged that were probably buried deep down somewhere, and the excessive amount of pressure from that "super experience" produced a different consciousness.

Comfort consciousness thoughts are the opposite of diamond thoughts. Receiving a healthy paycheck every week keeps people comfortable enough to where they don't feel forced to take the action to get them where they truly desire to be in life.

When you're making decent money and driving a nice car and live in a nice house, you're comfy. But are you living your unique success life of freedom? Are you financially free? A comfortable life will ground you; it's the opposite of what can produce diamond thoughts. When you're comfy cozy, you're not forced to think beyond your current circumstances. You're not forced to get creative.

CONSCIOUSNESS

After I went belly up, I worked the most creative deals I could in real estate. I was putting together unbelievable deals that I never would have done prior to my downfall because I was on easy street with the bankers and the money faucet was on and I had money in the bank. My crash changed all that. At the bottom, I was forced to earn my success from scratch. If you're at scratch, if you're feeling ultimate pressure, it's okay. In fact, not only is it okay, it could be the perfect catalyst that pushes you in a new direction—a direction you don't even understand yet.

Consciousness has different planes and levels. Your current consciousness could be two dimensional; but all this new information you are reading about could put you into a three-dimensional place, seeing things you didn't know existed. You don't know what you don't know; pressure-filled experiences can catapult you into exciting new thoughts and ideas.

You may be wondering, *Well, technically I'm not at rock bottom, I'm steadily in a comfort consciousness that isn't leading toward growth or anything great. How can I create an environment that is similar to extreme pressure circumstances so I can think diamond thoughts?*

That's a great question. A trick I use is to obsessively think about my life in the future and what it will look like if I don't do what I need to do. If I'm comfortable, I'm poisoning my urgency and diamond thought and creativity—my life twelve months from now will look exactly like it does right now. There will be no growth whatsoever. The key is to obsessively think about how painful your life will be knowing that in five years your life will be identical to this very second. All the advice about posting pictures on the fridge of a Ferrari and a mansion and looking at them every morning, squash that, okay? That doesn't work. That's simple-minded motivation.

Remember that preventing pain is a human's prime motivator, so focusing heavily on the pain of a stagnant life will get you going quickly. This is raw human nature. I hook into raw human nature because I believe those aspects of our beings are timeless. You're reading this book because you don't want to be in the same place five years from now, even a year from now; so if you can obsessively think about the pain of your situation, you'll take serious action. Creativity will flow. Diamond thoughts will rise in your mind. The diamond process will take over and it'll be like magic.

15

KEY SUCCESS MUSCLES

We all have "adversity muscles." Some of us have flexed them more than others. Flexing your adversity muscles can drastically enhance your future progress on your path to success.

When in my mid-20s, I built a very lucrative business and had a seven-figure net worth. In 2008, the national mortgage and housing crisis forced me into bankruptcy. I was broke, depressed, miserable, negative, didn't want to be around people, and was in a bad state of mind. It was hard to see any kind of light, because there was so much darkness.

Looking back and connecting the dots, I realize now how important that dot on my life timeline was. It caused me to flex my adversity muscles. Bankruptcy was such a catastrophic adversity in my life that it changed me significantly. Dealing with all that pain and tragedy back then allows me now to experience minor adversity much easier.

Now I operate with the mindset: "I've already been to the gutter, so whatever the world has for me, I'll get through it." Years ago, adversities and negative experiences made me crumble to pieces and freak out; today they are no big deal. The actual adverse events are the same then as today—but my *reaction* to the adversity changed.

ADVERSITY MUSCLE

My reaction changed because I flexed my adversity muscles massively during the downfall; everything was easier to handle after I took control of my perspective of the circumstances. The bar has been raised for what I can handle. I've seen the extreme, so most events I deal with now are below the extreme level, which means I deal with them with ease. Whatever the world has for me, whatever challenges are in store for me, I'm okay with it because I've seen much worse. There's always a solution, regardless the problem.

When you are in the eye of the storm, you can't really see a positive outcome. I tell people now that my bankruptcy and financial downfall was the greatest event of my entrepreneurial career. It produced a completely different person, a completely different entrepreneur, and a completely different mindset. It produced a completely different and deeper level of wisdom in me. My degree of perception is wide and my peripheral vision is clear. My view of my life is much sharper. I'm more open to evolving and not as set in certain ways.

The analogy of flexing your physical muscles is simple to understand. In weightlifting, the heavier the weights, the more pain is involved. But once you put those weights down, many other things feel really light. Make sense?

I encourage you to embrace adversity, because I can say with 100 percent certainty that you will be okay, you will survive, and you will become a better person after it's over. You will look back and realize the necessity of the experience for your unique evolutionary journey through life. As problems and adversities come your way, you will handle them with ease. Period.

It's a certainty that significant growth will come from extreme adversity. That certainty is timeless, it always has been true, and always will be true. Flex your muscles to the fullest. Look at tough times differently, understanding that you are being sculpted into a better and stronger human being.

This principle goes back to your unique evolutionary success path. Extreme adversity inserts certain markers inside your human experience that introduces other directions. A conglomeration of all the concepts presented can produce enormous success, and many times can quickly cause massive exponential growth.

DECISION-MAKING MUSCLE

The decision-making muscle is another crucial muscle regarding success in life. One huge issue preventing people from succeeding is indecision, whether small decisions or large. Some people obsessively ask so many questions about each decision that they cannot even take a minute step forward; and that's a serious problem.

Success involves constantly moving forward and evolving, whether you are right or wrong at the time. Not every forward step or forward decision you make is going to be correct in the moment. But remember, as you take those steps, correct or incorrect, you are moving. The beauty of making decisions is that you will develop the decision-making muscle. The more decisions you make, the better you will get, and the more decisive you will become.

Some people think that they are born either decisive or indecisive, that they can't control that part of their personality. But the reality is that being decisive is a skill to learn and develop. The more you do it, the better you get. Make a decision and move forward. The decisions you made that seemed incorrect at the moment, and maybe even were legitimately incorrect, will all be corrected as you look back, because those dots connected you to where you are right now. Make a decision with certainty and understand it's okay. Be open to looking at it, evolving, side-stepping, maneuvering, and adapting from there. Know that you're moving out of the stale state and into a place where you become more confident in your decision-making skills. If you don't conquer your fear of making decisions, you'll never get better at it. And life is full of choices.

When you have a decision to make, think, *I'm making this decision right now with all the information available, and if it's wrong, oh well. At least I took a step.* As you do that, subconsciously you develop a skill set that will move you forward. You will become better and better at making the right decision. Your decisions will become more and more correct in the moment, leading to a faster rate of growth. You have to make a conscious effort to decide to make decisions.

Some people have confidence issues that prevents them from making decisions. They think they have to have all the answers before they can make the right decision. They want to feel comfortable about the decision. The reality is, they will feel better and more confident about each decision they make as they make more.

Decision making is like any other skill set you develop. In the beginning, you may have to force yourself out of your comfort zone, then eventually it will become more and more natural. The more you do something, the better you get at it, and the better you get at it, the more confident you become. The more confident you become, the better results you get from the decisions. From there it is a very quick upward spiral working in your favor as you grow and travel along your path to success.

PROBLEM-SOLVING MUSCLE

Now let's talk about your problem-solving muscle. It's similar to the decision-making muscle, but there are differences. Problems are inevitable. Some people think that once they become successful, there will be less problems. Actually, usually the opposite is true. The difference between the successful and the unsuccessful? The successful have developed the problem-solving skill set.

As an example, I have dealt with lots of problems among many different levels of severity. As many business situations and problems as I've seen in all my years, new ones still appear. How can I solve new problems that I've never experienced before so quickly? I'm used to solving problems, so my mind is set in a state of finding solutions. I know I have the ability to solve problems because I have developed my problem-solving muscle. Because of my approach, I always find a solution. Period.

If you have kids, you probably encounter a new situation every day. Raising growing and evolving children consists mostly of maneuvering in uncharted territory. For me, when problems occurred when they were young, I didn't know how to handle them because the issues were brand-new. As my parenting problem-solving skills developed, I eventually could quickly and decisively come up with solutions. Even though the actual unique problem involved completely uncharted territory, I could engage my decision-making and problem-solving muscles to solve it. Many times those two muscles coincide.

Again, I want to make clear that the more problems you solve, the more confident you are in solving future problems. If you have a problem-solving mindset and skill set, it shouldn't matter what problem comes your way, because you're constantly building your muscle to solve problems—by making decisions.

Embrace the fact that problems will always crop up. Decisively solve each problem with confidence. Even if your solution isn't exactly on target, the fact that you corrected it in your own way is a step ahead, and the next time will be easier. In the beginning, I challenge you to get creative; come up with any type of solution you can think of. It may not be the best one, but the process of doing it is exactly the *best* thing for you.

For example, I'm not the greatest writer. But I put this book in your hands because I wanted to help people find success and change their lives for the better. My mission was to provide people with important information. Because I didn't have a lot of writing experience, I developed a different way to get these words to you that involved speaking, copying and pasting, editing, and rearranging things in a way that made sense to me using my unique strengths and weaknesses.

The solution was unconventional, but it worked because I'm fully aware of my strengths and weaknesses. Because all of my principles intertwine, I could create this life-changing core message I have for you; I created a solution. Who knows, in five years I may have a different solution that's better. But in the moment, I created a solution that worked, that's what matters. My own evolutionary path dictates changes I need to make along the way to stay fit and survive through the times.

USE IT OR LOSE IT

The physical-success muscle analogy is accurate. If you aren't using the muscles in your body, they are weakening. If you don't use your success muscles to make decisions, your decision-making abilities weaken. If you don't experience adversity and flex your muscles, you will have a tough time. If you are not actively making decisions, you will continue to have a hard time making decisions. No doubt you've heard the phrase, "Use it or lose it" referring to physical muscle mass. The same is true for your success muscles.

If you want to make better decisions, start with this daily exercise: quickly make small decisions without debating back and forth in your mind. Just look at the choices before you and say, "I'm going with that one," and settle the matter with extreme confidence. Over time, you will rewire your decision-making mindset.

If you are going through adversity, embrace it. Understand it is: 1) a temporary state, and 2) it's sculpting a better and stronger human being who can tolerate higher levels of adversity, getting through it with a calm and logical mind, as opposed to a freaked-out emotional mess that makes things worse. As far as problems, they will keep hitting you in the face. Take the blows, look at them logically, and create solutions. You will get faster and better. Eventually people will look at you and say, "Wow, you always have everything under control. Everything seems to go your way." Yes! Don't you want that? Of course you do.

Decision-making, problem-solving, and adversity muscles interweave to keep you strong if you keep using them. Stop being indecisive, stop wondering and worrying, just do it. The more you do it, the better you will get, and the more confident you will feel—a lot more good results will come your way.

When routine, daily decisions have to be made, consciously and quickly be decisive. For instance, when thinking about dinner, *Should I go out for Chinese or Mexican, or should I grill burgers at home?* Seriously, and I mean this with sincerity, say to yourself definitively, *I'm having burgers,* and cross the other options out of your head. You will become more decisive. Start with low-stake scenarios so when high-stake situations arise, you are quick and decisive. People around you will be attracted to your confidence, which brings your mission further, faster.

16

OPPOSING FORCES

You may face a variety of opposing forces to your success agenda. Let's examine what you may be up against, and continue to be up against, if you truly want success.

First, there will be individual naysayers and haters who can be spotted easily. They are inevitable annoyances for anyone climbing toward success. Climbers make them feel uncomfortable in their own skin. Their opposition is more about what's happening inside them, than about you. You are thinking on a higher level, taking more action and making new moves, and that doesn't jive with their mediocre mindset and comfortable lifestyle. They want to bring you back down to their level, and that's where the hating and sabotage starts. Your thoughts, ambitions, and ideas are not even the focus of their negativity toward you. It's them. Trust me; I've met more than my share of naysayers and haters!

Haters don't have the higher mindset that I've been teaching about throughout this book. They should actually be embracing the fact that you are taking new actions and climbing to new heights. They have a perfect opportunity to latch onto something positive and climb with you. But the sad reality is that most of the time it makes them feel very uncomfortable and feel less about themselves. Discomfort equals pain, so it's painful for them to see you succeeding, especially if you started from the same place and they don't have a valid excuse for not trying to get ahead. They will try to bring you down, negate your ideas, tell you what you're doing isn't going to work, or say, "The market's crowded. You're too competitive. You'll never break in. You're obsessed." These are just a few examples of what they may think or say to you, but the list is infinite. Be ready to deflect their negativity, politely. Then find other people to associate with.

Second, on a larger scale, conformity is the ultimate universal opposing force; conforming to the agenda at large. Remember that creating success usually requires breaking out of the "box" we talked about. Although there's no box for those of us who are evolving, opposing forces and conformity is society's point of view to keep everyone comfortable. The path to success opposes the universal umbrella agenda of the world. I read somewhere once that society as a whole works to build up an agenda that opposes its individual members. This really made a lot of sense to me and I realized how true it was. Society itself seems to be an oxymoron. Let's all get together to create something that destroys our actual individuality. Nonsense.

The robotic assembly line of people concept is ingrained in us from the day we're born. That's why I focus on more than just naysayers and haters in this chapter. There's a universal agenda that opposes people creating their own unique success path because that opposes society's need for nice and tidy conformity.

If you're doing what the masses are doing, you're never going to climb to success. You have to go where the masses are not and do what they are not doing. When the masses are opposing you and telling you what you're doing is wrong, crazy, incorrect, etc., most of the time it's confirmation and validation that you're on to something big.

In the early days of your success climb, haters and naysayers can be your fuel. The fact that they say you can't do it makes raw human nature kick in—and you want to do it that much more. What they are really saying is that *they* can't do it, so how can you? Your abilities are almost infinite, trust them to take you to the next level of success—no matter what they say.

EMOTION CONTROL

During your "immature" days of climbing, your emotions will attach to the scenarios when the naysayers attack you, oppose you, and negate your ideas. Your knee-jerk, emotional reactions are typical and you will be offended. But as you progress and mature on your success path, you can remove yourself from the scenario and see from a higher point of view, realizing they are the ones with the problems. You will come to realize that there's nothing inside you that needs defending. When you can understand that and become objective, you can walk away or simply respond intelligently. You must keep your emotions under control because reacting emotionally leads to arguments and negative events that will deter you. They will become defensive, and you will gain nothing by trying to convert them into believing in what you're doing.

Your time and energy is finite, don't deplete any of it on naysayers and haters. Don't spend brain power on trying to converting people who are jealous and envious. None of what they say to negate you is valid; you need to spend time and energy on creating your success. There are many other people in the world who will see eye to eye with you and make your encounters effortless. There are many people in the world who can't wait for what you're about to express through your success, so please don't waste your finite resources on anything else. You're not going to convert everyone; move on from them, period.

NO GRUDGES

Don't hold a grudge against opposing forces. Grudge-holding takes time, effort, and energy. There's no question about it. Holding grudges, especially against close family and friends, drains you mentally and sometimes physically. Psychologically, holding grudges and bitterness is very unhealthy. You can use those mental resources in much better ways while traveling on your success path. Let nature take its course with haters. Maybe they'll eventually evolve and see your vision and jump on board and be part of your team and support. Maybe they won't, but let nature take its course. You don't need to force anything on anyone.

Opposing forces can involve people in your life, even very close family and friends. That's where it can hurt us the most because we care about these people. But when you are staying in your own lane, focused on your success path, with mature, intelligent understanding they will no longer hurt or offend you. That mindset is easier said than done.

It took me many years to understand, but my evolution in that understanding has worked wonders for my personal success quest because it allows me to remove emotion and defensiveness from the equation. This is very important, because when you're operating defensively and emotionally, your logical mind gets pushed to the backburner. You start saying things you wouldn't normally say. You start doing things you wouldn't normally do. These events quickly build on themselves. It's like an addiction or any other kind of negative brain process. The situation will spiral downward very quickly, and you'll have a lot of ground to make up when you try to get back on your path. Don't focus on negative opposing forces.

A LIFETIME OF WEALTH

The success climb can be very lonely, because if you are going to become successful, you are usually doing something that the masses are not. Most people you know are part of the masses. For example, I started my climb in my late teens and early twenties in real estate entrepreneurship. That's when most people that age are partying, having fun, and not worrying about succeeding in their careers. They totally live it up.

Conversely, I had my head down and my focus in place to build a business. I knew that Social Security wasn't going to be there for me. I knew that I couldn't depend on any external source to produce a lifetime of financial freedom. And I also knew that because I was so young, I had the time and the energy to produce a business. Knowing that "you're only young once," it was the ideal time to create the foundation for a lifetime of wealth. My outlook on life at that young age was in opposition with my friends' views. Consequently, as I climbed the ladder of success, I had a lot of acquaintances; but as far as very close, tight friends, I didn't have many, because they had the herd mentality.

I was lonely at times because I was doing my thing when everyone else was doing something completely different. I didn't hold a grudge, but at times I did try to convert them to my way of thinking. I got into debates and arguments. My intent wasn't some sneaky way of selling them on my ways. I sincerely and passionately believed that I cracked the code on creating success and wealth. But I started to see that people weren't taking it necessarily the way I was conveying it to them. My excitement and passion weren't being well received. Then there was a threshold moment when I finally realized, "Wait a minute! I guess I'm just not part of the masses. I'm different and I need to accept that fact."

I knew I wasn't part of the masses, but a light bulb moment showed me very clearly that there are certain people who accept where they are and don't mind not growing. Growth and progress has been an obsession for me and served me very well over the years. I believe that continually advancing in life brings out the best in people and truly moves them into being more than average. Back then, I didn't believe in mediocrity and staleness, and I couldn't understand those who do. Now, as I write these words, I understand the other side, which allows me to work successfully with a variety of different personalities.

My early and continued success forced a lot of friendships to fade. This may become true for you as well. But your true friends and family will accept your vision and walk along with you.

17

RELATIONSHIPS

Relationships are super shortcuts to getting where you want to go when you're trying to create success. You can leverage and use other people's life experiences and compact your own. You can compact decades into months or years based on learning from someone else's experiences. That's why creating relationships is an important success key. But let's go deeper than that—who really cares about creating relationships?

Take, for instance, you attend a networking event and talk to someone for a half hour; you exchange business cards, and you're done. Forget networking—that's not creating relationships.

I'm encouraging you to establish and nurture real relationships. Having a big, fat Rolodex or hundreds of Contacts in your smart phone is worthless if the person you want to connect with is someone you haven't spoken to or communicated with in more than a year. It is totally unrealistic to think you call him or her to leverage your relationship a year later. It doesn't work like that. It takes time to nurture relationships. I'm a staunch advocate of staying in touch with people by calling to say hi or sending a fast one-line email, "Hi, how are things going? How have you been?" Connections matter—more than you think!

Going out to lunch or breakfast once in a while for real face time matters. Creating a bunch of relationships is worthless if you don't put in the long-term nurturing work. Nurturing is 90 percent of the relationship equation. A healthy relationship is give and take. Don't be a bloodsucker who always takes. Give, take, give, take—that's a real relationship. You have back and forth exchanges: conversationally, emotionally, physically, etc. You're always offering. Don't look for reciprocation every time you contact them, that comes the more you give.

Constantly fill the relationship cup. If the relationship cup is empty, it won't be a lasting and productive relationship. As long as you keep pouring in, it will stay full and both of you will enjoy the connection and be fulfilled. It may seem uneven at first, but in the long haul, both of you win with the right nurturing. The bottom line: once mutual nurturing occurs, you both will be able to leverage the benefits of the relationship and significantly shortcut your success.

If I can borrow a lifetime of knowledge and wisdom from someone who's in their 70s, I can't even explain to you how valuable that is. Yes, we need to attend the school of hard knocks. Yes, I believe in rough draft moves and getting whacked over the head and learning. Yes, it's important to back up, assess, and evolve—constant evolution. Combine all that with leveraging quality relationships and gaining wisdom from people who have been in places you haven't yet, these are the most valuable catapults in climbing to success.

"Leverage" is not taking advantage of someone or using them only for your own benefit. No. First you need to create a sincere relationship. Then reciprocation or "leverage" becomes automatic. That person can call on you in times of need and you can call on that person in times of need. If you're launching a new idea, raising money, or want a promotion within your company, your sincere relationships are going to drastically increase your ability to progress.

Leverage is not a sin in a relationship as long as your first goal and your first thought about the relationship is, "I sincerely appreciate this relationship, I'm sincerely going to nurture it, and I'm sincerely going to give when the other person needs something from the relationship." It's a two-way street. Almost all healthy relationships exist because both people give, but also receive benefits. There should be a zero exploitation factor in the relationship.

At the end of the day, people are in various relationships—business, social, emotional, spousal relationships—and most of those relationships are self-centered. People want to engage in a relationship so they can relate to another person in some way. Humans need and want to relate to each other. We feel good when we relate to others. I'm not talking about a sociopathic self-centeredness. I'm simply saying that most people want something out of relationships for themselves. But if you want to continue your benefit of the relationship, you have to constantly nurture and give; otherwise, the relationship will fade away because the person will sense self-centeredness and quickly walk away.

STRATEGY TRUMPS EFFORT

When dealing with career, business, and other professionals, you want to create strategic relationships. Strategy is part of the business world. Relationships can open doors for you that you could never open. A relationship with a certain person could give you access to ten doors that you will never have access to. Creating and nurturing that relationship in a sincere way is key. When you're working your way up to become a high-level executive or perhaps the CEO of the company where you are working right now, establishing good and nurturing relationships with people who are highly above you will enhance your ability to advance your career.

The reality is, advancements are not always based on merit. It's a relationship game more than anything else. I can't stress enough that strategic relationships in the business and success world are ultimate shortcuts to climbing high exponentially fast. The climb to success can't be done by yourself if you're trying to get to any high level. It takes a lot of hand shaking.

The foundation of my success is relationships. I didn't consciously decide: "I need to strategically meet all these people on my list, and I'm going to create success from them." No. The best relationships are organic and are naturally created when you have success on your mind.

Remember, be the person who is truly sincere and nurtures relationships. Send a fast text or a brief email something like, "Hi, just thinking about you. How've you been lately? How are things going?" That's a huge deal, especially in the fast-paced world we live in. The thought that went into typing those words that took you ten seconds is a seed for a volume of opportunity. The recipient thinks, *Wow, Nick was thinking about me. That's really nice.* This quick gesture on your part will stick in his or her brain because it interrupts the normal everyday pattern. It was interruptive. The brain remembers interruptions. That's how we're wired.

A month later when you call, that text or email will still be fresh on the person's mind. A positive communication. A lunch here and there just to stay fresh and keep things nurtured is very important. Put your ear into the relationship. Freaking listen. Understand who the person is; that's all part of the foundation of being sincere. Insincere relationships don't work. Creating relationships on the basis of extraction only is 100 percent failure. It will not serve your need or the other person's need.

People sense sincerity. As emotional creatures, we're wired to our senses. If you're sincere, your relationship will go a long way. Relationships are marathons, and the people who make it through, win. They shortcut the time required to achieve success; they compact decades of wisdom into short periods of time. No one wants to wait twenty years for success. Do you? I doubt it. You're reading this book because you want to create success as soon as you possibly can.

MENTORS

Everyone wants a mentor these days. As I've taught many people around the world about success, real estate, business, and entrepreneurship, I constantly receive requests from people asking me to be their mentor. Obviously my time is limited, but I do offer guidance and assistance when possible. This book is part of a mentoring process.

I have to say from experience that mentors sometimes have a selfish reason for mentoring. Many have an egotistical reason for mentoring. They like being the "guru" who can help people. Be careful who you choose as your mentor. Mentors don't want to be out-shined, which causes a problem for their egos; whether that's right or wrong, it's reality. Even if you grow to a very high point, you never ever want to come across larger than your mentor. This is something I've learned over the years with different mentors I've had. It's a strategic move and it allows the relationship to prevail healthily. The relationship demise can occur quickly if the mentor sees that the protégé is shining too brightly.

This isn't the fluffy sugar-coated book you may have thought it would be. This is reality, and I'm teaching you how to win long term. This is a small piece of necessary psychological warfare. I don't mean true warfare. I guess you can call it psychological strategy, but warfare brings up the point that there are two parties with agendas. Even if you are outshining your mentor, you need to put a shadow on the light when you engage personally with your mentor because it can cause a relationship problem.

THE 99/1 PRINCIPLE

The 99/1 principle has served me very well throughout the years. I am very open-minded. I have relationships with people from all walks of life. Not just the entrepreneurship and success world, walks of life in any world. Some of the best ideas come completely from left field, from somewhere least expected.

The 99/1 principle is pretty simple and just involves keeping your mind as open as possible when you encounter anything new. When I say open, I mean truly open to the point where you'll hear anything for a moment. For example, if you told me you flew to the moon with some special wings you built in your basement and now you're here to tell me what the dark side of the moon looks like and that you saw aliens, that sounds outrageous. But I'll sit down with you because it's new data that my brain never received before; and if I can pull out something new from 1 percent of that story, it would be worth the listen. If the other 99 percent is complete fantasy, fairy tale, laughable nonsense, I will have been entertained.

That's part of a relationship too. It'll entertain me and it'll be fun to talk about and BS with. If I can extract 1 percent out of that, and can somehow apply it in my life, the entire other 99 percent was worth hearing. That 1 percent could be a seed that sprouts exponentially huge when it's combined with my DNA and life experiences. It may be worthless in someone else's head, but it could be complete gold in my head.

When I look back at my life, there are many situations where I've pulled something out of complete left field that turned into something beautiful. It came from a completely different consciousness that was previously closed off to my mind. For example, I watched a show about alligators and somehow in the last ten seconds of that show something triggered my mind into a series of thoughts that allowed me to progress in a direction I never would have known about. I'm serious. The 99/1 rule, it works. Remember, the brain works in ways you can't even imagine. With the alligator show example, that 1 percent could be the seed to a mountain of new thoughts in your brain and thought patterns and directions for your next step in the journey.

I don't care if it's a bum on the street or a CEO of a company, your relationships with all people should matter. You should not necessarily seek out all strategic relationships. Relationships with people from all walks of life matter. It's the beauty of life. Connecting with them will produce thinking in ways that are way outside your tunnel vision. Your conversations will produce thought processes that you were never conscious of before. That goes back to my core message of how your evolution is exciting because it goes in directions that you can't project.

Let's go back to that alligator show for a minute. I would not be able to pull the 1 percent out of it without the proper psychological primer that says, "Great thoughts and ideas can come from anywhere." As you consciously start to look at things with an expanded mindset, more epiphanies will appear in front of you. I hope that at this point in the book you have expanded your degree of perception and primed yourself to be open-minded enough to meet people in all walks of life who will be the preface to beautiful thoughts based on the 1 percent you can extract from even the most obscure occurrence.

That 1 percent has carried the seeds of some of the most life changing shifts I've had. Those 1 percent scenarios have slowly expanded my degree of perception of life in ways I can't even put into words. Albert Einstein said that "No problem can be solved from the same level of consciousness that created it." That fact correlates to what I'm sharing with you. The way you think now will most probably be completely different five and ten years from now. That truth intrigues me. It's so exciting to know that the 1 percent can change everything.

18

STRATEGIC LEADERSHIP

Leadership involves strategy. As you climb toward success, you will inevitably be in leadership positions either within the company you work for, or your own entrepreneurial endeavors. You need to know how to lead and manage people. Leadership is tougher than the business you're in. If you're an accountant, you can be a great accountant, but if you want to build an accounting firm, you have to learn how to be a quality leader, which is a completely separate set of skills. If you're good at laying concrete, great, but if you want to build a concrete company and do big commercial projects, you have to have people working for you. And you have to motivate them, inspire them, and get them to do things to better themselves and your company vision, which is the key.

Leadership begins with knowing some basic facts such as there's a lot of different personality types. Over the years

I've learned how to deal with many different personalities and how to get to the core of how they work. When you can understand personality types, you can understand how to engage them in certain ways. I believe there is no umbrella leadership statement where someone can say, "This is how you manage people: step 1 is this, step 2 is that, step 3 is that." No. There are way too many unique scenarios.

I'm a big advocate of putting your senses deeply into the relationship to hear and keenly observe how people operate so you can act accordingly. I've managed some people one way, that I would never dream of managing someone else the same way. Leading may be intimidating if you have never have managed anyone, and I totally get that. Fortunately, if you truly and sincerely observe people's actions, words, movements, and their intentions through conversations, and ask the right questions, leading well will become more comfortable and happen quicker than you think. It's not something that takes decades to master.

If you're trying to build a mission, business, your success platform, etc., you need to involve and then lead people if you want to grow anything of real size. You need people to grab hold of your mission and your vision. Here's the thing, you need people to *want* to be part of your vision. If you have to force them to be involved, it will be a short-term relationship.

If you want to be a true leader, you have to discover the true intentions and aspirations of the people you're leading and reasonably cater to them. If you can do that, whether it's money, incentives, freedom of creativity, freedom of thought, freedom of input, etc., they will be loyal and will work hard for you. Multiple things drive people. The end-all is not always, "I'll give you raise." It's not always financial. It's part of the equation, but people need to know that you truly appreciate what they do, that they are an important part of the business. If they feel that, they will plug into your vision and your vision will flow and grow—they'll *want* to be part of it. If you're looking to be a long-term leader, you need to understand your people.

EGO-DRIVEN

Many people who worked for me over the years had ego problems and were arrogant. To me, those are the easiest people to lead and manage, because their drivers are very clear and they wear it twenty-four hours a day. Every word and movement they make is based on projecting how great they are. A lot of it is obviously rooted in poor self-esteem, so they're constantly projecting a high self-esteem. That's Psychology 101. I cater to their ego. I affirm their egotistical behavior because it inflates them and allows them to feel good about themselves. If you show them that you're holding them in high regard, they are some of the most easily managed people in the world. This isn't manipulation, this is how leaders adapt and evolve based on who they're leading.

Remember, though, you don't have to be best friends with the people who work for you, you just need to maintain a win/win relationship. Realizing that ego-driving people are in a permanent state of mind where they have to constantly be proving themselves, they are very easily managed; all they want is confirmation about how great they are. If you can give that to them, they will be good workers for you.

QUIET PERSONALITY

Some people are not conversationalists, they're very quiet and reserved, and they don't like to talk about what's on their mind. It is best to know how to lead these people because although mostly quiet, some of them will of a sudden do something drastic. I've encountered this situation several times, and I would be totally blindsided when they quit or had a serious confrontation with someone—or me. Many times I was left in the dark wondering, *Wait a minute. What was that all about?!* They never engaged me in conversation and explained how things were.

Now, as soon as I recognize someone who is quiet, I immediately approach them over a cup of coffee to pry information out of them with questions. Some people offer all the information, some remain more reserved, but reaching out to them shows you care. That's why I believe egomaniacs are the easiest people to manage. They wear everything about them on their sleeve (so to speak). They show people who they are verbally, physically, anyway possible.

The quiet people are harder to understand. It's best to sit down with them and say, "Hey, tell me what's going on here." You may have to loop back around multiple times to actually receive some substantial information. Don't pry in an annoying way, but routinely and regularly ask how things are going, intentionally triggering conversations. "Hey, what you think about that new procedure? What do you think of that?" Ask specific questions. "What do you think about the timeline on your project?" He might have a concern about the timeline and give you important information about the project. Quiet people don't outright tell you the information you need to know—you have to ask.

But with quiet people, don't ask, "How's it going?" because they're going to say, "Good," ten out of ten times. "Good" is a dangerous word with quiet people because all of a sudden they may explode, and you have no idea why. I learned that the hard way before I finally realized that I had to initiate conversations to head off an explosion of negativity.

GREAT LEADERS

Great leaders strategize how to best cater to their employees (and even volunteers) to ensure loyalty and long-term commitment to your mission and vision. If they're working for you, the likelihood of their mission trumping or crushing yours is unlikely, so you don't have to be insecure about that. If they are super ambitious, they can grow with you; if they branch off and do their own thing, so be it.

The people you lead need to enjoy what they're doing and feel happy about it. Some people may be in positions that don't fit and they aren't happy, but you can point out all the benefits and place incentives for them within reach to brighten the picture. Obviously, this doesn't work every time, but it will weed out the people who are miserable and aren't assets to the business. Not everyone will be leadable by you, and that's totally ok.

TRUE LEADERS PRODUCE LEADERS

True leaders produce scenarios where people are happy doing what they're doing and eventually become leaders themselves. Priming new leaders is part of leadership. People enjoy being leaders. People enjoy management. People enjoy being in charge. Raises and bonuses are only part of the incentive equation. People want autonomy. They want to feel in control and become a manager and leader. Giving them some space to do that produces a new quality feeling that is part of their life mission of being a leader. Not everybody wants to be a leader, but those who do will excel if given a chance. If they can't handle it or things go wrong, you can have them step back, take a deep breath, assess and continue to evolve perhaps in a whole new direction—which goes back to a lot of my other principles shared previously. True leaders can produce other leaders if leadership is part of their vision.

I've seen many people become extremely happy and productive when put in leadership roles in charge of certain people, projects, timelines, or whatever. I could sense the joy coming out of their pores; they were so grateful to be put in that kind of position, their sense of accomplishment exploded. This enthusiasm will trickle up into your main vision.

Being a great leader means you have to be sincere. Not everyone is cut out for it. The reality is, yes, you will have to fire people; yes, things aren't always going to work out, but that's part of the evolutionary process. That's part of rough draft moves. You plug people in, and if they don't work out, regroup.

I believe that leading people into their own evolution is the epitome of leadership. Lead people into the evolution I talk about throughout this book. Lead people into their own success path that looks like success for them. If you can lead people into their own personal success, which plugs into your own vision—that's the ultimate win/win leadership scenario. Everybody is happy in the relationship, and it perpetuates positive, forward direction for all involved.

19

GO MACRO IN TIME AND SPACE

I encourage you to "go macro in time and space." Another way of putting that is to "zoom out." Zoom out and get the full landscape view of your timeline and also your current, exact place in space. It's definitely easier said than done, but it's something you need to do to truly understand your mission on a larger scale.

The more you zoom out and go macro in your space that you're in, the more you're going to be able to see, the more you're going to know how to deviate and evolve and adapt based on everything you're seeing. Really what I want you to do is expand your degree of perception.

Also, zoom out on your timeline. Make your vision of your timeline timeless. Just because something has always been, doesn't mean it will always be. I like the statement,

"We only know what we know right now." What we know right now produces a "take-for-granted arrogance" that what is will always be.

When people woke up in New York City at 6 a.m. on September 11, 2001, life was a certain way. Three hours later, life was totally different for them and people worldwide. That's an extreme example, but we only know what we know right now. Everything could change in an instant and if you look at time based on a higher degree of perception, you can maneuver more successfully and make much wiser decisions.

Consider the collapse of major empires in history. If we were to talk to the leaders of those empires a short time prior to the collapse, they would never have been able to foresee life outside of them ruling the empire. They would have laughed at someone who told them what was about to happen, convinced that things would remain a certain way; they knew no different. We only know what we know in the moment.

But when you zoom out and go macro on timelines and realize that what is true for today may be completely untrue tomorrow, you will be in a place of power in your pursuit for success because you're open to a lot of change very quickly. True succeeders and innovators today understand that tomorrow could bring things that today can't even imagine.

Some beliefs and convictions I had ten years ago, aren't even close to those of today. That's healthy because it means I'm evolving and growing. I will continue to keep a macro view of my timeline. Picture a timeline and you slowly living life throughout it with the beginning being your birth and the end your death. Then imagine the power of being an eagle looking down at you while walking your timeline of life; you can see the whole thing. This presents a different perception of time and the macro scale of it.

LOOKING AT LIFE OBJECTIVELY

It's hard to see objectively what's currently happening in your life because you're so emotionally immersed in it. Time passing will help you see more objectively, but right now you may not be consciously mature enough to understand what's actually happening. For example, as I look back at all that I've been through in my life, the dots fully connect. But you may only see your current dot (on your timeline) and not necessarily see the connections yet. That's why it's so important to be as objective as possible—so you're not totally blinded by the moment. That way you can see more connections and really get a grasp of how far you can go.

Since it's so hard to be completely objective, you may need to have a close family member, friend, or mentor look at your timeline. They may see patterns and connections that you may not see, which will help you determine your future dots. Understand that when you're on a dot, it's just one dot in a long line of dots. When you look at the time-line from a macro point of view, you won't place much importance on one dot, especially if it's a negative scenario, because you realize that there are many positive dots in the past and the future. Immature minds get stuck on the sad or tragic dots. Believe me, I was guilty of this for a long time and it's not an easy transition. But the macro view shows you a completely different picture of your life timeline, showing you how all the dots connect in a beautiful way, moving you along—past the bad times.

To fully get the benefits of a macro view, it may be wise for you to hire a coach or somebody to present this scenario to you. It takes mental maturity to get past troubled times and move forward along your life path. Zoom out and see everything in the big picture—the entirety of your life, don't focus on the minutia of the moment.

Another example: letters versus words versus paragraphs. When young, you learn the letters in the alphabet. Soon after, you are spelling words. Then you zoom out and are stringing words together that make sentences that are grouped into paragraphs. After that, you've created an entire story. One letter (aka one dot) means nothing. One word within a sentence has no meaning. Even one paragraph within the entire story may have no meaning. But reading the entire story makes sense. You need to understand the context of your story in time and space.

CONTEXT AND RELATION

Everything is contextual. Your timeline and your point in time and space are relative to other points of time and other points of space in your path, in the world. Looking at life this way allows you to see things that you wouldn't normally see, and you can prevent problems and catastrophes. You can enhance your exponential growth to where you want to go and enhance the ability for positive things to come your way. More opportunities will be realized when you zoom out and look at the big picture of your timeline and the big picture of space around you.

This macro approach to success is timeless. No matter the economy, the political worlds, whatever technology is built around us, if all of that is removed from the equation, the lessons and ideologies taught in this book will prevail. Apply these principles, and your personal and unique evolutionary success path will continue to evolve.

We only know what we know right now (worth repeating because it's an extremely important realization), and we take things for granted way too often; we have to realize the constant natural evolution and changing world around us. A zoomed out, macro approach to success allows you to thrive in any scenario, in any era of time, and with any type of technology that comes and goes.

20

BECOMING A SUCCESS SCIENTIST

I believe that in order to succeed at your maximum capacity, it's imperative for you to become a scientist. What do scientists do? They study, they experiment—and sometimes things blow up in their faces. They observe what works and what doesn't. As you experiment and observe what works or doesn't work, as a success scientist, you will experience more and more "light bulb moments" times when all the components fit together perfectly and you are successful. Scientists are trial-and-error masters, and that's the way you must approach your success path.

When you tackle problems and challenges along the path and things don't go the way you planned, put your ego aside and try again. Acknowledging the wrong way to solve the problem forces you to search for a deeper level of understanding, and then your next effort will be successful. When you think you know it all—that is a poisonous state of mind. Wrong isn't failing. Wrong forces growth, and progress, and more learning. You should always be on an obsessive journey to learn, if you truly want to be successful.

When things go wrong, take a step back and ask yourself, *What could I have personally done differently to prevent that from happening?* Examining the situation will hone and sharpen your skill sets even more. Although you will have others who assist you along the way, being self-reliant is important. When you operate from the point of knowing you have all the power to create, maintain, or destroy your success, that is a special place that allows you to go much further.

Listen, nobody in the business world cares about you—except those who depend on you for their profits or products—suppliers, customers, etc. No one is going to give you a hand out, no one will give you a break. Nobody is going to make you successful. You must be the catalyst to make it happen; don't depend on outside forces.

SELF-RELIANCE

Self-reliance is a very helpful trait—maybe the most important. Many times scientists work alone—each focused on his or her own particular task. They can't depend on others because others have their own task to complete.

In the business world, most, if not all, have their own agendas and goals and views, they're on their own paths doing their own thing. Yes, there are sincere relationships that you will cultivate and nurture throughout your years; but in general, adopt the understanding that nobody is looking out for you, and you must look out for yourself at all times. It's true personal accountability and responsibility.

I've pondered my past business mistakes in great detail to learn from them, and I have extracted massive amounts of wisdom. There were many things I could've done differently. I can't blame the economy; I am a self-reliant human being, and I am my economy. I want you to be your economy, as well.

Yes, there are some strong external forces that can sway you in one direction, but that's when you adjust your sails and use every ounce of self-reliance to navigate through the rough waters that can and will approach you at various times in your life.

If you force yourself to look inward and examine your motives and your perspective, you will always have a clear view of how to create growth and see opportunity. Pointing the finger at yourself is an opportunity. Accepting responsibility for fault can present infinite opportunities that most immature minds don't consider. It puts *you* in control, instead of depending on external circumstances to go your way.

Let's say you're in a very competitive industry, and the economy's booming, and everything is going well. While your competitors are flying high and their egos are also flying high, you should be asking yourself, *How can I evolve from this up-swing? What next steps do I need to take to keep the momentum going?* You will exponentially climb higher than the competitors, because you are continually self-examining, which is imperative to progress. When things are hot, that is a perfect time to buckle down and really grind, because when things cool off (they always do), you'll be light years ahead of complacent competitors. Strike when others are sleeping in current bliss.

Taking an objective approach to life and business, no matter how good it is right now, is a very important point. There have been times when I was so sure about something, then all of a sudden, the smallest issue tilted my perception and then it spilled over, and my whole viewpoint changed for the better. A whole new floodgate opened up. This actually overlaps my 99/1 rule. Being 100 percent closed-minded and dead set on a certain tactic, strategy, or whatever is not healthy. If you keep an open mind, the smallest of issues can change your viewpoint, exposing you to possibilities that you didn't even realize existed. Being dead set on something today, could look ridiculous to your future self.

Fear influences greatly how we operate in general. Being open-minded scares people, because they are very comfortable with what they choose to be dead set on. Fear substantially hinders real growth.

SKILL MASTERY

As a success scientist, it's important to know what skill sets you currently have and some you don't. You need to gain mastery over your current skill sets. Don't develop your weaknesses; develop your strengths. Put every ounce of your soul into your strengths because that's from where true greatness emerges.

There is something very rewarding about mastering a skill. Instead of doing something all day, every day to master a skill, I figured out that if I do something in short bursts, I can master a skill much more quickly. In fact, there's science that backs up my claim; it's how the brain learns. I take laser-targeted bursts of action, then walk away from it, allowing the neurons to connect. Then when I go at it again, with the new burst of practice, there's a sense of flow that occurs as the skill develops. I don't believe you need ten thousand hours to master a skill. Try quick bursts, over and over, often.

You pull the rabbit out of the hat by mastering your strengths. Mastering your strengths produces greatness. Success is a combination of nature *and* nurture; you're born with certain genetic strengths, and then you're nurtured into, or out of those, and maybe nurtured into other strengths. Becoming self-aware and understanding what abilities you already have and then nurturing and fine-tuning them—that's when you create "magic" in a variety of scenarios. Be your own magician.

And while on the topic of magic, during my teenage years, I loved the idea of being a magician, and doing tricks. I met the owner of the local magic shop, who had been a magician for fifty-plus years, and we became buddies.

Practice Strategy

He introduced me to a few tricks; and out of all of the magic, sleight-of-hand is what attracted me most. He gave me a book about card tricks, which I read, and then practiced a couple of tricks for short periods of time. I would be obsessively immersed, using100 percent of my brainpower in practicing the tricks. Then I'd stop and go back to it later, or the next day. I think my brain needed the break to catch up with the intense, laser-targeted practice time. It needed to weave together the skill in its web of neurons. I wasn't born knowing any magic skills, but I had an interest, a seed of desire. In the moment, I wasn't aware of the process I was using to create the skill quickly, but looking back it's very clear to me.

After showing my magician friend the tricks I learned, he said, "You know, you really have a knack for this. You really have a special ability." The reality is that I didn't have a knack or special ability, I practiced in a very specific way. It was great to hear that from a long-time magician, but all I care about is how I view it now, from my lens, so I can teach you.

Accidentally, I figured out the magic ratio in the brain of how much to practice and how much to break after practice. The brain needs to rest and connect the new pathways that are created when learning something new. Let the pathways have time to connect. It's like a muscle. When a muscle tears when lifting weights, it needs to rest to let it repair and grow. I believe the highways and learning passages in the brain are no different. Again, at that age, in my late teens, I had no idea that was the science behind it, but looking back, it's clear.

Another example is when I started piano lessons. I never had an interest until I was in my 30s. But I decided one day that I would give it a try because it intrigued me. I learned the same way as when I learned magic tricks, I practiced in short obsessive bursts, walked away for a while, then did it again. My teacher, a veteran piano player, said, "I think you're very musically inclined, you have a knack for this." No, I don't. I'm not a musically inclined guy. I quickly gained a skill based on a process that I accidentally discovered. Perhaps you can learn a new skill using my technique. It certainly is less daunting than believing you have to spend months or years to acquire a new skill.

The success path skills I've learned are no different. The *quality* of time is very important; it trumps the *quantity* of time. Commit to full immersion mode when you are practicing. Involve your whole mental capacity. I believe the best learning comes from immersion. Your brain has crazy amounts of power, and if you give 100 percent of it when you're learning, you'll be shocked at how fast results appear. When you are fully immersed in whatever you're doing, even if it's for a short period of time, the results can be tremendous. This should be your approach to mastering whatever skills you want to learn.

Immersion

An example of immersion working beautifully is learning a foreign language. If you are dropped into a foreign country, you're immersed from all angles in that foreign language and culture. Eventually, grasping the language will be natural. You will learn the language the same way you learned your first language—through immersion. Immersion is nature's true way of learning. Immersion affects the conscious and subconscious; you don't have to study and memorize.

Relating to business, immersion helped me when I first started in real estate. I feared dealing with home sellers, not knowing exactly how to communicate so I could put good deals together, especially because I was so young. I didn't how to talk to them, what to say to them. Rapport-building is an important and necessary skill in your climb to success, and I didn't really have it. I could've read about rapport, which would've helped, but rather I immersed myself in talking to people, practicing building rapport firsthand. I forced myself to make friends with random people wherever I was. It became something I consciously did until it eventually became an unconscious habit. After a while, it felt normal and natural. Because I was constantly in an environment of building rapport with people I didn't know, I mastered the skill.

With immersion, you don't have to read about it and memorize different techniques and tactics, because you're immersed in the scenario that you're trying to learn. The brain brings in immersion data different from reading a lesson about the topic or memorizing strategies. The key to gaining the skills needed for success as quickly as possible is to learn it, then immediately jump into immersion. It's the way the brain works.

Studying world history is important. It reveals what people in previous civilizations did, could've done, or should've done differently to survive. History reveals a 100 percent objective scenario, because we look at it through an impartial perspective. If studying human history, world history, and geographical history is so important, it make sense to study our personal history to learn from it, right?

LEARNING FROM YOUR PERSONAL HISTORY

Scientifically break down your history from right now and trace back as far as you can remember. Ponder all the dots on your timeline, see what has connected and what hasn't. Part of being a success scientist is realizing that history truly repeats itself and can predict the future. Seriously examining your personal history and your family's history is highly recommended and should not be overlooked.

After you truly become conscious of your personal timeline in history, your conscious mind will expand to viewpoints you didn't even know existed. Looking back, you can dissect different scenarios in your life, in your family's lives, and understand them. Rather than taking for granted who you are, reflecting on your history may point to who you're going to be. Gaining that conscious understanding through the scientific method of dissection, study, and experiment will expand your view of yourself and your family.

For example, your father may have worked twelve hours a day, six days a week, and he ingrained in you that hard work is the only way to succeed in the world. That outlook has a long-lasting impact on the way children look at their work lives. Analyzing and studying those types of past scenarios will be very enlightening in assessing your worldview now.

Study your family's history like a scientist, truly dissect it. I'm sure it will make an impact in your understanding of where you can, and will go, moving forward.

21

DETACHMENT

When starting from scratch on your way to success, you will encounter various bumps in the road. Negative scenarios will arise as you pursue success. It's not a secret that there is a true climb and uphill battle toward success. I'm sharing as much strategy as possible because I want you to win and I believe that strategy trumps effort. When you combine strategy and effort, you have a winning scenario.

If you let the inevitable bumps in the road flood you with negative emotions, your brain will start embedding beliefs that the failures are permanent, that you won't be able to do it. You have to detach yourself from negative emotions and maintain a logical mindset. Emotions spiral much quicker than logical thoughts, especially negative emotions. One negative thought spirals into two negative thoughts and then more things attach, and pretty soon we're quickly at the bottom. That's why it's important to remove emotion from tough events.

Removing emotion from an issue isn't easy, especially in the beginning when you're new, but force yourself to zoom out and objectively understand the scenario—look at just the facts, which allows you to stay focused on your path. Without emotional involvement clouding the way, you will see the end goal and what you're working toward. Remember, tough times are just part of the journey. It's okay to step onto the path knowing that you may be clobbered and beat over the head sometimes.

Changing your mindset and detaching emotions must be a conscious effort in the beginning. All change involves, first, recognizing the scenario. I think one of the main reasons people don't change or get stuck in negative patterns, is because they don't know it exists. I feel badly for people who haven't had someone wake them up to it or they haven't run into enough scenarios to wake themselves up to it—in the beginning, it takes real effort. Step one toward success for an addict is raising his or her hand and saying, "I am an alcoholic. I am conscious of my problem."

Step one to changing negative emotional patterns is to recognize the problem.

Step two: after you recognize your tendency to be controlled by negative emotions, when miscellaneous scenarios arise, be aware immediately and consciously change your mindset. Detach yourself from the negative emotions bubbling up inside. That's how habits are formed. You may mess up sometimes and react negatively, but as long as you make a conscious effort to detach from negativity, it will become easier and easier and your behavior will change on an automatic basis, unconsciously performing positive habits.

Sever the emotional link. Detach your emotions from negative events; emotions are the strongest force of our behavior. If you create negative emotions that are attached to negative events on your path, you may form some very limiting beliefs that you view as reality. When, in all reality, it's actually imaginative thoughts that are being tightly wired for your disservice and your demise.

Let's discuss ego attachment. If your ego and entire emotional identity is attached to your success, if you have a severe downfall like I did, it also brings down your identity, your self-esteem. It brings you down because you've attached too much of your self-worth to creating success. On the flip side, it's just as important to detach your ego as you become successful. Giving too much credit to yourself makes you arrogant and when the inevitable downturn comes, you will be devastated. Don't attach your personal identity to your success or your failures. You are *not* the actual events of your life. I hope that makes sense to you.

When you preserve your unique identity, you have the freedom of knowing that no matter what happens, you'll be fine and will bounce back. You are learning not only how to create success from scratch™, you will know the way to create success after having a major demise.

I've done this twice—once from zero and the second time after a complete financial demise and bankruptcy downfall. This detachment lesson allowed me to go a long way very quickly because I maintained logical thinking throughout my climbs and kept my personal identity detached.

I really want to drive this home with you because if you do completely fail or an opportunity you're pursuing goes completely south, it's just *that* particular opportunity. It's just *that* business deal that failed. Each of those is only a micro event in your macro world. If you attach your identity, your ego, and your self-worth to one event, it will destroy any ounce of personal power and self-esteem inside you. Again, the only reason I'm able to teach this to you is because I've been way up, and I've been way down—I've seen what dragging your personal identity up and down can do. I've seen what emotional attachments can do to people on the up and down side; therefore, it's very important to operate from a higher perspective and a higher objective.

Detaching emotion from micro events—negotiations, business discussions and deals, etc.—allows clear thinking to make logical macro decisions in your favor.

22

ACCEPT UNCERTAINTY

Let me start this chapter off right here, plain and simple. When you can be open to whatever happens to you, including severe devastation, negative events, micro-failures, getting hit in the face, etc., that is when you will break into the true and liberating freedom of the world of success. Your fears will disappear and you will welcome all the magic that happens in the uncharted territories in your life.

Throughout history people have accomplished many unbelievable things, feats that defied what was thought possible. We will continue to see that. Accepting the fact that you don't know the future is the mandatory threshold to cross to tap into your own infinite capabilities. The fear of the unknown paralyzes most people. *Uncertainty creates fear, but it also creates the most success, if you accept it.* I firmly believe that stepping over the threshold takes you to where the real magic happens. Think about it. If you just trot along the timeline of life walking only in charted territory you're familiar with, you will never get different results. It's common sense that isn't quite so common these days.

I'm *not* saying you should dive into everything head-first, knowing nothing, and then get beat up knowing that it's going to be okay. No. I'm saying, gather and study some quality info and then make some moves, even though you don't know what the exact outcome will be. Make a move knowing that you can always step back and reassess.

Using this method over the past years makes life so much easier and peaceful; and I've made more progress, because I know I'm stepping forward. When I make the wrong move, there is freedom knowing that it's going to be okay, which drastically minimizes stress and eliminates fear. I just reassess, evolve, and move forward. That's how you win. That's how you make real progress.

Everyone has something inside just waiting to be exposed, exploited, and used to fuel us into new and exciting areas of life—places we dream about. Accepting uncertainty knocks down any monster brick wall holding you back. You need to destroy the wall by accepting uncertainty. Choose to be aware of the walls you've built—then knock them down brick by brick.

You must be able to accept total devastation—which could be right around the corner. You must know that you'll live through it if it happens. I can say with clarity, it's never as bad as you think. If you can accept that it could happen, you have freedom and power to win that much more. When you don't go after everything you're capable of, you're never going to fully win or feel fulfilled.

When playing a sport, I've heard it said, "Play with heart and leave everything you have on the field." It's the same with a successful life. If you're scared about what the opposing player might do, automatically you won't be in your full "A" game. There's nothing more fulfilling than playing a sport to win and putting everything into it. It's the same with success. I'm not saying total devastation is something you should yearn for—but it is something you need to prepare yourself for—mentally and emotionally. If you lose the "game" (business failure, bankruptcy, loss of job, etc.), you can fall back on realizing the liberating freedom of power of knowing the game was just a road bump on life's path. It was a micro dot on your macro timeline.

By now you've realized that perspective, perception, and what lens are you looking through allows you to become successful naturally, and you see the world as one big opportunity.

CREATORS AND CRITICS

At this point in my life, I teach people how to reach success using proven methods that worked for me. I expose myself to the world knowing there are critics and people who ridicule what I do. There are creators and there are critics—and creators attract critics. When you become a creator, don't sit around and theorize all the things people may think about you. Rather, focus on your lane and moving ahead. You have to be okay with the fact that there will be opposing forces, opposing people, ridicule, negative comments, etc. Allow these deterrents to give you freedom and power to attract people who will support you. There is much power in truly embracing the idea that uncertainty is completely okay.

It's in our nature to want to be certain of things because being certain of things, thousands of years ago, meant life or death. It's part of our wiring that we have to work with, evolve out of, and think ourselves away from. Certainty doesn't mean life or death anymore.

Let's examine the "certainty" of the higher education myth. Society teaches us that if we earn a higher education degree we are certain to get a job, certain to make a good living, and certain to retire comfortably. While I don't oppose higher education, I do believe it is a myth. A higher education does not guarantee certain success. Many, many people have become very successful without a college degree—especially in this era of technology where there are infinite entrepreneurial opportunities.

For those who buy into the higher education certainty myth, they may end up with a decent job that produces levels of comfort that actually hinders their ambition, preventing them from pursuing their real success dreams. They may be doing something they "kind of" like, when they could be doing something they love, but the certainty and comfort of their position keep them from going after their passion project, even on the side. Their hunger is dulled by comfort. Then in five or ten years they think, *Wow, I wasted so much time. I'm still doing the same thing when I could've been climbing toward my dream life of success.* Certainty is an aspect of that vicious default cycle we discussed previously.

There have been unprecedented changes that happened very quickly in this current technology era. We only know what we know at this instant. There is no certainty of anything that's to come. As much as we analyze and prod at the facts and theorize, true, 100 percent certainty, doesn't exist.

Not stepping into uncertain territory jails you in a boring, dull cell for the rest of your life. You will never defy the odds. You will never break out and shock the world. You will never do anything great as long as you need to be certain. Accepting uncertainty is the ultimate foundation of all growth and success.

23

ROUGH DRAFT MOVES

"Rough draft moves" is a core concept that I embrace daily and have taught to many aspiring, successful people worldwide as part of my mentoring career. Absorbing this concept into your mindset separates those who succeed from those who don't. Fact: to advance in life you have to make a move. It doesn't have to be the correct move. A move, no matter what it is, is the foundation of progress; even if 99 percent of the move is wrong, you are still progressing. If there's a shred of anything right, simply extract it and correct the 99 percent with the next rough draft move.

Don't look for a finished product in the beginning. Start with a rough draft move. People who win and succeed continually make rough draft moves, leaving everyone else in the dust who are still theorizing.

Rough draft moves involve pre-action and post-action analysis. Pre-action analysis is analyzing a theory, which is nothing more than a bundle of neurons in your brain coming up with an idea. There is no validity at that point because it hasn't been projected into reality. Rough draft moves take whatever is in your head and makes it reality.

For example, writers and painters whip up rough drafts and sketches the moment thoughts comes to mind. Most of it is probably junk but they move forward by taking the step to get their ideas onto paper and canvas. Later they extract some of it, evolve the thoughts and ideas, make improvements, then craft another draft.

We can look at life as one big manuscript or one big blank canvas. So, live it so people will remember you. That's another whole side topic. Write and edit, correct mistakes in your life as you go along. You don't need to know the ending, just write the rough drafts, take action, then cut out what isn't right or healthy and keep the rest, adding to it daily with new and exciting experiences. Rough draft moves are the foundation of taking something that's in your mind and making it real and tangible.

Don't allow pre-action analysis to evolve into full-blown paralysis and obsessing about things that aren't real. Rough drafts take the unreal to real. After taking action on your rough drafts, then you can assess through post-action analysis to see what worked and what didn't and make adjustments. The only data that matters is actual data taken from actual action. Theoretical data in the climb to success is mostly a meaningless series of thoughts, triggered from fear and imagination.

A certain amount of pre-action analysis is necessary; of course you shouldn't bet the farm on something you don't know much about or invest your life savings in something on a whim. But you can take an initial action—a rough draft action—knowing you can analyze it later and assess the outcome. Taking action is foundational for growth.

You have a finite amount of time and energy and brainpower as you move along on your path to success. You need to invest most of that time, effort, and energy in making rough draft moves so you can move exponentially faster. You will come to know what parts of the rough draft need to be dumped totally and what parts are worth pursuing. Spending too much time analyzing wastes time. Step out of that mode and into the next productive day and be more positive. Don't be like a kid scared of what's under the bed with too much pre-action analysis. Stop it.

Likewise, with post-action analysis after your rough draft moves, you realize that constant modification and evolution is part of the process of climbing higher. Then, as you make new rough draft moves and make appropriate modifications, you can look back at the trail you are forging and see major progress!

ROUGH DRAFT MOVES...

Making rough draft moves open doors that you don't yet know exist. There could be twenty-five doors waiting to be opened from a rough draft move that isn't even in your realm of consciousness. Making a rough draft move shifts and opens your perceptions and consciousness to things you don't understand yet, things that aren't available to you yet. Rough draft moves produce the infinite. Rough draft moves can take your life in positive directions. Rough draft moves will put you in touch with people you don't know who can help you immensely. Rough draft moves should turn into your new healthy obsession. Rough draft moves put you in monstrous positions to go places you can't fathom right now.

If you don't make rough draft moves, many of these new doors may shut by the time you get around to walking through them. Many could have timelines that expire while you're too busy in pre-action analysis or trying to talk yourself into moving beyond your comfortable zone. I'm sure you can think about all the moves you didn't make but wish you would have. You wonder what opportunities were left on the table because you didn't make the move. It may make you sick to think about it, so don't think about it too long.

If you truly retrace all the steps and all the pre-action analysis you took, what is left on the table is literally infinite because of the directions things could have gone. On top of recognizing and being aware of pre-action analysis and post-action analysis, get used to constantly taking rough draft moves. All those future opportunities will be yours for the taking.

Rough draft moves are like snowballs. They start out small but exponentially grow and grow. If you continue to obsess on pre-action analysis, you leave success and opportunity behind. You want to get to your goals fast, right? I'm with you. You don't need twenty years to make your dream a reality. If you take strategic rough draft moves on a regular basis, you have the world in your hands.

TAKE ACTION

Everyone has great ideas. But many of the greatest ideas, songs, poetry, music, books, are buried six feet underground. Period. Ideas are worthless unless take action on your ideas—make your ideas real. Many great ideas are buried because people obsessed during pre-action analysis and never did anything more, so they took their ideas to their grave. They didn't make that first rough draft move that could've opened doors to cure cancer, solve poverty, or bring about world peace. We'll never know.

Successful people take the time to make responsible and reasonable calculations before making a rough draft move. In a painting example, you choose the right brush to draw your rough draft move. A writer would first choose to write a novel or a text book. Don't act completely crazy or irresponsible to the point where your moves make zero sense.

A business plan is part of many businesses. It sets out the future strategy, goals, operation, and financial development of a business. It is a theory about what could happen in reality. It's an extension of an idea. You don't need a perfect business plan to be successful. Some of the best businesses and the best success stories in the world were never put on paper.

I've been good at making rough draft moves, quickly assessing them with the resulting real data, then moving forward to the next step. I've had multiple successful businesses and I've never put a word on paper in a business plan, ever. I'm not saying business plans are worthless. I'm simply saying that obsessing about a business plan and perfecting it is just another form of pre-action analysis that paralyzes you.

Success from scratch belongs to people who have a track record for constant execution and rough draft moves. The person who jumps into something and knows how to quickly adapt and evolve will win. Constant evolution and adaptation is crucial.

REAL-WORLD DATA

You can be a PhD candidate and write a killer thesis paper on creating success from scratch, but if you've never done it, it's simply a theory. I like to operate with data I produced with real-world actions to accomplish real-world goals. Theories can be great in their place, but when you're trying to truly climb, spending effort on theories wastes time—and many doors of opportunity may close.

Rough draft moves is a simple concept: you make a rough draft move, you screw up, you sidestep, you adapt and evolve. You make another rough draft move, eliminating the missteps; it may still be rough, but a bit more polished. So you sidestep and adapt again until it works perfectly—or until you scrap it altogether. Rough draft moves is a rinse-and-repeat process.

President Abraham Lincoln said, "Give me six hours to chop down a tree and I will spend the first four sharpening the axe." I understand why he said it, and I always appreciate wise words from a wise person, but I'd like to offer another perspective using the rough draft moves ideology. If someone hands me an axe and says, "Cut down that tree,"

I don't know what kind of wood it is. I don't know what kind of tree it is. I don't know how old or healthy the tree is. I don't know the density of the wood. All I know is I have an axe and the tree in front of me. That's reality. What if I don't need the full six hours? What if I swing the axe one time, a rough draft move, and get half-way through it because it is an old, rotted-out tree? Am I really going to tie up four hours sharpening my axe before I swing it for the first time? No.

I say, swing the axe first; the entire tree may fall, or maybe the axe goes through half of it, or maybe the axe barely makes a dent. After that initial blow, you can then make an intelligent decision about the next step. The Nick Ruiz quote is, "Give me six hours to chop down a tree and I will first swing the axe once to assess the need to sharpen it."

Rough draft moves is a core concept in my life and something many people I've mentored and helped have latched on to. For more information about this important success concept, visit SuccessFromScratch.net.

24

YOU, INC.

You are a business. Everyone runs their own personal economy whether they like it or not. There is a top line amount of what you bring in and a bottom line that is left over after bills are paid, etc. Even if you don't think of yourself as a business, in a sense you are. It is best to have a profit every year, but with credit card purchases, car loans, and home mortgages, many people never even break even at the end of each year. Eventually, their financial demise may be a mathematical certainty.

Most people look at money only as currency with which to buy products and services. Wrong. Money needs to be strategically deployed in the world, almost like soldiers, creating total freedom if used and moved the right way.

Most adults mismanage their financial resources. They've never been taught how to create wealth and financial stability. Most students don't learn about financial management in school, which has led to debt and financial turmoil. Our country is currently $19 trillion in debt—not a good example for the population.

First, creating financial independence and wealth has *nothing* to do with how much you earn and *everything* to do with what you do with what you earn. Over the years as I earned significant amount of money, I allocated funds in the proper direction that allowed me to grow my wealth and financial independence.

Financial problems cause divorce, addiction, and many other negative things. Financial stress keeps people up at night and can make people physically sick. You are a business and are responsible for the funds that come in. You can't just point your finger and say, "Well, the government did this and my money manager told me that, and this is why I'm broke." You can point your finger all day long, but at the end of the day you're still broke—so what are you going to do about it?

You need to take control of your money and understand where to best allocate your funds. You bring money in, you manage your resources accordingly, and you either are in the black or in the red at the end of the year. That's what business owners do. You are no different. Start with developing a budget, being conscious of your costs. Fixed costs and expenses occur every month regularly. There are also sporadic unfixed costs and expenses.

BUDGET TIME

Following a budget, like all successful businesses do, is the first step to personal financial success. Businesses have regular meetings to review expenditures. Your meeting should be with your spouse if you are married, or by yourself if you're single. There are hundreds of sample personal budgets on the Internet you can use as samples. It is important to write down every amount you owe, when payment is due, and what is the interest you are paying on it. Include incidentals such as food, gas, dental check-ups, etc. Until you know what expenses you have, you can't control your resources. Also, write down your income. This important step may be a huge wake-up call when you compare your income and expenses on paper.

Successful businesses don't just wing it when it comes to money. They strategically and regularly monitor their resources, allocating them appropriately, eliminating unnecessary expenditures, and making moves and investments where they think their return on those investments will be beneficial—you are no different.

PROTECTING YOURSELF

In a traditional business, poisonous employees, colleagues, or associates can cause a company to go bankrupt. Poisonous people don't have the company's best interests in mind, rather they seek to undermine and corrupt. They must be cut out. Throughout my entrepreneurial career, I've had to cut out many poisonous people. I do so quickly now before they create a vicious environment.

You are no different. You need to cut the poisonous people out of your life. Just like a bad manager can destroy your business, a bad close friend, family member, or colleague can destroy your personal life.

MARKETING YOURSELF

A business becomes successful by attracting and keeping people's attention through marketing strategies. To be successful, businesses must capture customers' attention, no matter if a restaurant, an online business, shoe store, grocery store, etc. When people are attracted, they enter the store or website and interact, hopefully purchasing the products and services offered.

Whether you're trying to grow a career in the corporate world and climb the corporate ladder, or starting a business of your own, you must attract people's attention. You don't have to be some hotshot, obnoxious person who blabs 24/7. That works well for some people, but being yourself and presenting yourself with confidence is best. Being aware of yourself and your strengths and weaknesses is key.

Some simple ways to get attention: consistently stand out by giving extra value, such as completing a project early and telling the boss that you are ahead of the game. Perfect little example. Make people think of you as more than part of the crowd. Do things that will make someone bring you up in a conversation. It doesn't have to be monumental; a lot of small things can add up to people talking about you. "John has been performing at an excellent level." Or "Mary's reports are top-notch, very professional." That type of attention-getting works in the corporate world, but as entrepreneurs we need to use the online world to our advantage. Use all of the social media venues available. You can reach thousands of people you will never meet in your lifetime.

EXPOSE YOURSELF

Everybody is unique. You have something inside that can benefit the world, but if it lies dormant and unknown, it's worthless. You can add value to the world if you expose your product or service in a way that people will want to receive it. Nobody cares about you just like no one cares about businesses. What they care about, mostly, is themselves. How will your product or service benefit them? How will it make their lives better? How will it add value to their lives? Only you can display yourself appropriately and accurately.

Grab people's attention by being an anomaly. Reveal your unique value proposition. The brain stops and notices anomalies because they stand out from the crowd. You won't stand out if you're doing and saying the same things everyone else is. You have to present something different, something new and exciting—you.

There are many people trying to promote themselves these days. The crowd is enormous. Remember our first conversation in this book about the new herd. Consequently, you have to say and do something different. You don't have to stand on top of the Empire State Building and scream. You don't have to do anything extreme or dangerous. You just have to be your unique self. Your unique DNA and unique life experiences are your ace in the hole.

No worries. It's not a problem. Just creatively get yourself out there.

25

GROWTH AND ADVANCEMENT

This topic focuses on when you want to grow, scale up, be promoted, or build your business. Each of those desires are attainable, which requires work on your part. It's worth the effort, trust me.

There are two kinds of work—linear and spherical. What's linear work? Linear work is two-dimensional. It's a straight line. It's technical work. It's something that any trained technician can do. Going back to self-awareness and realizing where you're strong and weak, if you really want to grow your business, you need to delegate tasks that are linear such as accounting work, technical tasks, office work, etc.

What is spherical work? This is where you shine—it's the passion that launched your dream to start your business.

It's what you're great at and allows you to continue growing your vision. Spherical work involves your creative ideas and your visionary thinking. While you're busy working your craft in the spherical realm, because you have delegated, all the moving parts in the linear realm are working at the same time. This is how you scale up. It won't work any other way.

Let's use the example of my real estate business, managing construction projects, and things like that. I'm good at finding deals. I'm good at building rapport with sellers and buyers and making deals happen. I'm a deal maker and a people person. I'm very good at salesmanship and persuasion. What I'm *not* good at is painting, refinishing hardwood floors, installing cabinets, accounting, those kinds of things. Do I understand them fully? Of course, but it's linear work that others can perform better.

Spherical work is like your entire business is an actual sphere. There are infinite points in space in any and every direction where you can land and create a new thought or explore a new product or service. Linear work is going from point A to point B. But you, as the leader, are going to operate in the infinite sphere, you're operating in the higher realm of strategy and creativity in your craft.

There's an expression, "As an entrepreneur you should be working *on* your business, not *in* your business." That sums it up. If you're trying to build your career, you should be working on your career. You have to be working *in* your career but you also have to be working *on* your career.

As soon as you can get some traction in your success climb and can delegate, I highly suggest you do because it will expand your time to do what you do best—making things happen strategically.

You are the general. Generals run the show and lead strategically. This is where you need to spend most of your time. When first starting your business, you can't delegate because you probably can't afford to. But once you're there, realize that you're the chess player, not a chess piece and you have to act accordingly. You purchase more time by delegation because as you pay someone to take over a linear position, you can do what you do best and grow your income exponentially.

Most people trade their time for money. They do work and get paid. But when they stop doing work, they stop getting paid, and they trade their time for money. I want you to trade *money for time,* that's what I alluded to in the prior conversation. You're building a business; and when you're getting some traction and income, you need to immediately start delegating people to linear tasks, which purchases you more time. Paying people just buys you a ton of time to start operating on a grander scale and moving forward on bigger, more creative projects, and more growth. If you're tied up with linear technical jobs, it will bog down your brain and deplete the finite brain power, energy, and time to where you won't be able to grow like you want to grow.

STRATEGICALLY ALLOCATE RESOURCES

Another strategy I've learned and used over the years, especially in the early growth stages, is knowing which bills have to be paid on time and which ones can be paid late without consequence. Some expenses can wait and some can't. As they come in, you prioritize them and pay what's necessary, then take the leftover dollars and invest in yourself; you can always go back and pay the remaining with new funds received.

For example, as I continue to build my rental portfolio, a stack of property taxes may be received. If there's a deal on the horizon where I could get a nice return on my investment, I may tie up my capital in that deal knowing I could make ten times the money back in a year that it would cost me to pay the taxes late. That's a simple example of many. You have to weigh those situations and determine where your dollars would be most strategically allocated, and place them there.

Paying yourself and reinvesting in yourself first is what matters. You don't want to incur severe penalties against you and you want to play by the rules, but if you can maybe swallow some late fees or some penalties knowing that putting your dollars in another place will be worth ten times what the late fees are, you're making the smart decision. If the return is larger than the interest or late fees, it's the right move to make.

Income can cure most things; climbing upward quickly is your ultimate defense as much as it looks like offense. You may be thinking that your growth and higher income is offense, but as you gain momentum and grow, you are also *defending* yourself against the threat of a competitor. The faster you grow and the more sales you bring in, the more you are insulated from competition hurting you. When you have a very strong top line, it makes the flow to the bottom line much cleaner and softer, and bumps in the road are less painful. "Top line" is gross revenue, the total money that comes in the door. The "bottom line" is what's left after all expenses.

Another important factor to understand as you grow is that you will encounter a more elite group of competitors and the rules can change. In a previous chapter I talked about the fact that "All you know is what you know right now." Here's a perfect example. You have gained traction, you're a rising entrepreneur, things are going well in your business, but as much as you're opening the doors to new opportunities, you're also opening the doors to new competition and problems, which will result in new rules. Rules that apply now may not have applied before.

One last thing about competitors. I'm not one for heavily focusing on competition because I want you to stay in your lane and not be distracted. Just remember, if you are constantly climbing and growing and being very strategic with your time and money, competitors are going to be much less of a worry. Like I told you, you're actually defending your business along with being offensive in your growth.

26

THERE ARE NO RULES

The statement "There are no rules" mirrors the chapter about how there is no box to think outside of. Rules were put into place by someone who saw a gap and said, "We are going to make a rule about this." Laws of the universe can't be changed. Rules are made up by people. "Rules are meant to be broken" is a simple-minded expression and I'm not suggesting that it's a blanket statement. I'm simply saying that what's in *your* mind is just as valid for creating a new rule for your life, as the person who created the rule that supposedly opposes the thing you're trying to do. I hope you fully digest that.

There are written rules and there are underlying and unspoken rules that most people in civilized society live by, such as not walking across the street until the walk sign blinks, returning books to the library, etc. There are certain guidelines you need to follow to be a good human being in the world.

But other rules such as the high education myth discussed previously is not a rule. It's a process that someone made up and may work for some, but it's not the *correct* path for everyone. It's something that someone thought up a long time ago for actually their own benefit. If you really want to break down how that school system was set up, it started back in the industrial age. It was made for their benefit to produce more factory workers, but the point is, many rules were made up for the creator of the rules benefit and no more, so it's okay to raise your hand and question things. As long as we're not doing things that question our integrity or break the law, you may need to break some rules to get where you need to go.

Your thoughts are valid. You came up with them out of your unique DNA and experience structure inside of you and 90% of people shoot down those thoughts because there is some rule in place. They think, "well who am I? *'They'* must be right because they made the rule." Again, if they dug deeper into what I just talked about, that rule was there for someone else's benefit or just because they saw uncharted territory in the world and said, "Let's make a rule about this". The person that made this rule is a human just like you, so why would that rule be more valid than what you're compelled to do?

Whether it's a person who thought of the rule or some big large organizational agenda that thought of it, the point is that it probably it was made for their benefit more than anything else. It's really a shame how many people reverse their pursuits of success based on these rules that they think are concrete and some kind of law.

As long as you're doing something that you're passionate about and feels good to you, and coincides with your internal world and your belief system and you're compelled to do it, do it. Regardless of what "box" it doesn't fit into because as we talked about earlier with the box in that chapter, there's nothing to fit into. There's infinite space everywhere for anyone to do anything they want and there are no true molds that anyone can, or even should, fit into.

You are your own mold. Everyone is an anomaly. You're unique in your own way and you just have to embrace your inner anomaly and also project it out to the world so they can see it, appreciate it, and understand it.

All the rules and structures that are in place around you right now are relative to something else. Most of the time what it's relative is to just the fact that it was on chartered territory at some point. Remember, everything that we see around us was just a thought in somebody's mind. If you look around the room you're sitting in right now, everything you see was once looked at as impossible.

Your pursuits can lead you to the infinite, but sticking with the norms, the rules, the supposed rules of engagement of this world, will 100% crash that pursuit and will lead a miserable life because of the fact that it's not going to coincide with who you are. Too many people in this world are miserable because what they're doing every day doesn't coincide with who they are and they're going in a violently different direction than what their inner being is telling them. That's a depressing place to be. It's a dangerous thing for this world because more and more people are becoming miserable and the epidemic of depression, anxiety and misery in this world is spreading like wildfire.

The rules that were made that make you think that your pursuit impossible or unachievable, are made by people who are just human beings trying to figure out their own way through this crazy world and they don't have it all figured out either. No one does. These "rule-makers" are just trying to make their way throughout their blink of a timeline in this infinite universe. It's amazing to me how many people put so much weight on these "rules". They're all just people. I don't care how successful or unsuccessful they are. I don't care if they're blood relatives in your life.

Understand that if the neurons that are wired in your brain produces these thoughts, ideas, and pursuits, they are valid and they are just as valid as all the things and people you hold in high regard.

As you pursue these things that you're compelled to do inside of you, more and more ridicule and opposition will be in front of you. As you pursue your dreams, opposition engages. I want you to be ready for it, but I also want you to just realize in the simplest form that this opposition isn't valid in your world. It may be valid for them, so let that live and die in their world and take no part in receiving it. For you to embrace their worldly thoughts and perceptions for your own life is absolutely ludicrous and will hold you back in ways you can't even imagine. So it's my goal and intention for you to make the rules for your world. There are no rules except the ones you create for yourself. I believe that with my soul. Those are the only rules you need to operate under and nobody can tell you different. I'm obsessed with the idea of there not being any rules and I can show you many more examples of the benefit of this thinking over at SuccessFromScratch.net

CONCLUSION

You have a unique DNA structure and a unique experience structure. That combination is one in infinity. Comparing yourself to others and how they do or don't do things has nothing to do with you. This truth has been repeated throughout this book, because as soon as you embrace that fact, along with the other principles, you will on your way to creating your own evolutionary path to success. If you are obsessed with what others are doing, you will move up the ladder in slow motion. Time is too important for that.

Your success starts within by recognizing who you are, your strengths, your weaknesses, and letting the evolutionary path roll out before you. I agree that picking up bits and pieces of wisdom from successful people with different strategies and modeling successful people is beneficial, but *your* success path will not be identical to someone else's, so let your internal world navigate you and be your own GPS for your own path.

Comparing your path with someone else's will interrupt the flow of your organic evolution, which is very unhealthy. You won't create the true results you want if you go in directions that are against your being. Life is short and every person has a unique opportunity and a unique ability to put a dent in the world, small or big.

One of the main missions of this book is to help you expose your uniqueness—not to "hype you up," but to get down to the core of who you are, shed what's wrong, and build up what's right. Then you can project everything you have to offer to the world. This world would be a much better place if more people revealed their real selves. My philosophy goes beyond the simple, "Hey, I want you to make a million dollars!" I want to make a collective, positive impact in this world with these writings—through you.

FREEDOM

Freedom is when you have choices, you have time to do what you want, when you want, how you want, and with whomever you want. If you want choices and you want time, you have to purchase both. You want to create success from scratch within a business or career, which is great because embracing all these principles and ideologies will get you there. There is no question about it, because you now have the right psychology to thrive anytime, anywhere, in any industry, any economic environment, etc. You're rising above all micro-scenarios and stepping into a huge macro-success environment that trumps all.

When you achieve monetary success, you become financially independent, which means you can purchase your choices and your time. Make no mistake about it, those are actual cash purchases. If you want to do what you want and have choices to make, you have to write a physical check. That's the way this world is structured. At a different point in time, things weren't necessarily like that, but the way civilization has evolved, it takes money to get freedom. When you have freedom, you will smile more, and when you smile more, other people smile more, and the domino effect of happiness continues. Again, that's the general mission that I'm trying to accomplish by this book—making the world a better place.

You may have never been exposed to this kind of material. Maybe you grew up in a family construct that thought completely different. Maybe you grew up in a negative environment. Maybe even after your childhood, in your adulthood, you've been surrounded by harmful people who shut you down or put you in a corner to cry. I'm here to say that's all okay. The beautiful thing about the way our brain is structured and wired, and the beauty of the human being in general, is that our current situations can be changed in a very short amount of time.

You can create an entirely new legacy for your family—one past generations have never experienced. Actually, scientists today are studying epigenetics, a field I'm in no way an expert, but am interested in. Epigenetics is the study of heritable changes in gene function that do not involve changes in DNA sequence; the study of the way in which the expression of heritable traits is modified by environmental influences or other mechanisms. Changing the way your mind operates moving forward from today can affect your kids, your grandkids, all future generations on a biological level. You can create a whole new family legacy starting today. That excites me for all the people who have tragic family histories.

You can consciously engineer a whole new breed. It's okay if you came from crazy scenarios and negative circumstances. Even though you may feel backed into a corner and you hate to wake up and face the world every day, I'm here to say it's okay. That feeling is not permanent. In fact, it's extremely temporary; and within weeks or a few months from now, your entire life (and the lives of your descendants) can be totally different.

HAPPINESS

You can create a whole new perpetual cycle of greatness and happiness over and above any type of monetary success that you can gain from all this information. The reason you want financial freedom is to purchase time and freedom and choices. You want that because it's going to make you happier. People just want to be happy.

There are simple, two-dimensional acts of writing down goals, hustling hard, waking up early, and staying up late to reach your goals, but the two-dimensional approach doesn't have any type of depth of impact that my three-dimensional principles and ideologies have. They go to the core of who you are and they can be projected to the infinite ends of the world. They're truly what it takes to make real changes in your life. Yes, you have to do some of the simple things, but then you have to go way deeper and way beyond so you can be the greatest person you can be to create success for the rest of your life and impact others.

Once you awake to who you are—all the things you need to shed, and all the things you need to consciously develop in yourself to create your own evolutionary path—that's the first day of your success journey. That is when it begins for you, and that's an exciting place to be.

You know by now that I've created success multiple times. I've experienced failure. I'm a twice self-made entrepreneur. The reason I can write this book is because I've obsessively looked back at how I created my successes and how the failure happened. I dissected each step because I wanted to make sure no matter what the economic circumstance was, no matter what the industry changes were, no matter what happened in the world externally, I knew I had what it took internally to create success again and again.

The byproduct of my obsession—this book, for you. Your personal journey to creating success from scratch can start today. These principles put into practice can keep you secure and successful for the rest of your life. Even if something happens and you lose it all, you will be able to duplicate it again. Success is all about your internal world. I've proven it, there are other people who have proven it, and now that you've read these words, you're going to prove it too!

Many people ask me questions like, "Hey Nick, what should I do? I'm 18 years old. I'm about to graduate high school. What should I do with my life? I don't really want to attend college. I really have a dream and passion about (fill in the blank)." Listen, the bottom line is: you're in a wooden box 6 feet underground for eternity. When you truly view your questions, life, things you're scared of, and all your uncertainties through the mindset of that box in the ground for eternity, you will see life through a whole new light. You will realize that everything you're worried about is nothing. All the questions keeping you up at night will have clear answers that start to appear. Your life span is a blink of an eye; why do something that makes you miserable?

Let's take the 18-year-old's question as an example. My answer to that young person, "Does your passion require you to go to school, for example, to be an architect, an accountant, etc.? Or do you want to pursue an entrepreneurial career and start your own business such as organic farming or designing and selling handcrafted jewelry? Or how about that killer offer from a great company that's developing a new musical instrument that you're excited about. You're 18; do what suits you now. You're young, number one. And number two, even if you're 40, go for it! Remember, you're in the ground forever. Do what's going to make you smile today and then be open-minded throughout all of tomorrow's possibilities and opportunities."

SUCCESS FROM SCRATCH™

People want to be successful—success means different things to different people. Only you know what success means to you. I hope you're excited about implementing the ideologies and principles in this book! *Success from Scratch*™ will bring success, which will make you happy. Happiness is the common denominator for all you will achieve.

Looking within and determining your North Star is the best advice anyone will ever give you. Realize that one day you will only be a photo on a shelf, and use that thought to guide you toward what's important and what will make you happy long term. Even the hardest questions that paralyze you right now will become easier to answer. That's when your true, unique evolution will begin. Fear will destroy your unique evolutionary path of success. But if you use my analogy as your North Star, fear will fade as your dream emerges. I hope you will begin your unique journey today.

Remember, there's no such thing as "10 steps to success," and then you're successful. My goal in writing this book is to reveal the life principles that allow you to attain success. I hope by now you have shed all of those embedded "get success quick" concepts that are destroying your possibilities; I hope you start to consciously build the internal world that will roll out the most beautiful red carpet to the most beautiful places for you to achieve your desires. I don't want this conversation and connection with you to stop here. Please visit SuccessFromScratch.net where you can get in touch with me and read lots of other cool content about your climb.

Remember, your journey will not be identical to anyone else's; but guess what, that's the beauty of the whole success scenario. Because it won't look like anyone else's, it'll be your own unique stamp on the world, it will be a reflection of who you are. Your ultimate happiness and fulfillment in life will be in knowing that you built your success from scratch—in your own way and on your own terms.

Celebrate!

DEDICATION

This book is dedicated to my 3 daughters Sofia, Sabrina, and Aria. I love you girls more than you could ever imagine and I want this book to be an example that you can do ANYTHING in your lives. Hard work and dedication to building your dreams will give you so much fulfillment and happiness. There is nobody that can tell you what you can do in your life except yourself. Listen to your inner voice, trust yourself, and never go against who you are or what you want for ANYONE.